STUDIES IN THE REIGN OF
TIBERIUS

STUDIES IN THE REIGN OF TIBERIUS

Some Imperial Virtues of Tiberius
and
Drusus Julius Caesar

BY

ROBERT SAMUEL ROGERS, PH. D., F. A. A. R.

PROFESSOR OF LATIN AND ROMAN STUDIES,
DUKE UNIVERSITY

GREENWOOD PRESS, PUBLISHERS
WESTPORT, CONNECTICUT

The Library of Congress has catalogued this publication as follows:

Library of Congress Cataloging in Publication Data

Rogers, Robert Samuel, 1900–
    Studies in the reign of Tiberius.

    Bibliography: p.
    1. Rome—History—Tiberius, 14–37. 2. Tiberius,
Emperor of Rome, 42 B.C.–37. 3. Drusus Caesar, 13
(ca.) B.C.–23. I. Title.
DG282.R6 1972   937'.06   77-152601
ISBN 0-8371-6036-7

To

D. E. T. R.

PREFACE

The Johns Hopkins University honored me with an appointment as Lecturer in Latin for the academic year 1939-1940. In discharge of the grateful obligation which that honor imposed I presented on 12, 14 and 16 February, 1940, three lectures on " Some Imperial Virtues of Tiberius." It is my hope that these essays may be of interest to a somewhat wider audience, and perhaps make a small contribution to the better understanding and greater appreciation of Tiberius and his government. They are printed here substantially as they were delivered.

Invited to read a paper before the four hundred eighty-seventh meeting of the Philological Association of the Johns Hopkins University on 15 February, 1940, I offered some excerpts from a study of " Drusus Julius Caesar," which has engaged my attention intermittently for several years, and which is now presented in its entirety.

To the many friends, old and new, who made my visit at the University so enjoyable and so richly rewarding I wish here to express my thanks, and most especially and particularly to Professor and Mrs. David Moore Robinson.

I am indebted to old friends and former colleagues for aid generously extended: to Professor Kenneth Scott of Western Reserve University, for helpful criticism on some problems in the study of Drusus; and to Professor George Eckel Duckworth of Princeton University, who transcribed the texts of several inscriptions not accessible to me. I acknowledge also very gratefully the expert assistance, in the description of Drusus' appearance, of my colleague in the Fine Arts department of Duke University, Miss Alice Bradford Robinson.

The passages quoted from the Loeb Classical Library are reprinted by permission of the President and Fellows of Harvard College.

ROBERT SAMUEL ROGERS

Durham, North Carolina,
March 28, 1942.

CONTENTS

a.
"Civitatibus Asiae Restitutis"
Liberalitas

b.
Rudder and Globe
Providentia

c.
Clementia

d.
Moderatio

a. From Bury, Cook, Adcock, and Charlesworth, General Editors, *Cambridge Ancient History*, (Cambridge University Press, England). By permission of The Macmillan Company, publishers in U. S.

b. From the *Römische Mitteilungen*.

c, d. From the *Journal of Roman Studies*, by permission.

SOME IMPERIAL VIRTUES OF TIBERIUS

I. *LIBERALITAS* AND *PROVIDENTIA*

In the Roman Empire certain qualities and characteristics of the ruler are personified and celebrated as manifestations of his beneficent governance of his subjects. Some such abstractions are consecrated as divinities which then receive temples, statues, altars, sacrifices and dedications. One will recall at once the golden shield which Augustus proudly records was presented to him in recognition of his *Virtus, Clementia, Iustitia,* and *Pietas*: one will remember the temples of *Concordia* and *Spes,* the altar of *Pax Augusta,* the dedications to *Securitas Augusta* or *publica* or *temporum.* These imperial virtues and sanctified abstractions are commemorated in loyalist or adulatory authors, and sometimes in hostile but honest writers; they appear in inscriptions, official or unofficial; and those of which the individual Emperor was most proudly conscious, or which were part of his imperial programme, so to speak, were frequently propagandized on the coins which issued from the mint to circulate among the population of the Empire.

You would perhaps be more ready, more sympathetic, to consider the imperial virtues of Augustus, of Trajan Optimus Princeps, or of the Antonines. But if you are initially disposed to deny Tiberius possession of imperial virtues, I beg you to withhold too hasty judgment, but rather to study with me some aspects of the history of Tiberius' principate.

It may again strain your indulgence that I propose to commence with *Liberalitas,* since you will doubtless re-

3

member the contrast between the lavish and frequent shows and games of Augustus and his successor's aversion from presenting or attending such entertainments;[1] perhaps, too, Suetonius' statements of his parsimony,[2] and the fact that by careful and consistent economizing he left behind him a large treasury surplus to be dissipated by the extravagances of Gaius.[3] Or again some may perchance recall the story told by Seneca in his essay on *Benefits*: "Tiberius Caesar, asked by Marius Nepos to rescue him from debt, bade him supply the names of his creditors. . . . When they had been supplied, he wrote Nepos that he had ordered the money paid, adding some offensive advice. The consequence was that Nepos had neither a debt nor a benefit; Tiberius freed him from his creditors, but did not bind him to himself. . . . That is not liberality, it is censorship. It is assistance, it is a subsidy from the Emperor; but it is not a benefit, because I cannot remember it without blushing."[4]

Yet *liberalitas*, or its synonym *munificentia*, does occur not infrequently in our sources for Tiberius, and many passages in which the word is not explicitly employed describe actions of Tiberius which may properly be referred to that virtue—benefactions to individuals, to whole classes of the population, to cities in the provinces, and extending over the whole period of his reign.

---

[1] Tac., 1. 54. 3 f; 1. 76.6; 4. 62.3; (references to Tacitus not otherwise specified are to the *Annales*) Suet., *Aug.*, 45; *Tib.*, 47; Sen., *de Prov.*, 4. 4; but cf. Dio. 57. 11. 4 f.

[2] Suet., *Tib.*, 34. 1; 46. (References to Suetonius not otherwise specified are to the *Tiberius*.)

[3] *Id.*, *Cal.*, 37. 3; but cf. Balsdon, *The Emperor Gaius*, 180-189.

[4] Sen., *de Ben.*, 2. 7. 2—8. 2. Translations not acknowledged to the Loeb Classical Library are my own.

At his accession when Tiberius paid to the troops the legacies of Augustus he added like amounts as donatives.[5] To each of the nine thousand soldiers in the praetorian guard was paid then a donation of a thousand sesterces, half that amount to each of the three thousand men in the urban cohorts and three hundred sesterces apiece to some 125,000 legionaries and an indeterminable number in the volunteer cohorts of Roman citizens.[6] Here was a largess upwards of twelve million *denarii*, or considerably more than two million dollars gold. Suetonius, after recording that donative, mindful no doubt of the frequent and repeated bonuses of Augustus and many of his successors, says of Tiberius " nihil umquam largitus est " except that after the suppression of Sejanus he paid one thousand *denarii* apiece to the praetorians because they had not adhered to their prefect, and " quaedam munera " to the legions of Syria which alone of the army had not worshipped Sejanus' effigy among the legionary standards.[7] What " quaedam munera " amounted to, it is impossible to say, but there were four legions in Syria or some twenty thousand men; the donation to the guard, at any rate, was another million and a half of gold dollars. Finally in his will, following Augustus' example and in the same amounts, he left legacies to all the troops with the addition of the seven thousand men of the night watch whom Augustus did not remember.[8]

We hear of only three *congiaria* (although Velleius writes " quotiens populum congiariis honoravit ").[9] In

[5] Suet., 48. 2.
[6] Tac., 1. 8. 3; Suet., *Aug.*, 101. 2.
[7] *Id., Tib.*, 48. 2; cf. Dio, 58. 18. 2.
[8] Suet., 76; Dio, 59. 2. 1-3.
[9] Vell., 2. 129. 3.

A. D. 17 when Germanicus celebrated his triumph, Tiberius in his name made a viritane distribution of three hundred sesterces to the populace.[10] Three years later the young Nero came of age, and in A. D. 23 his brother Drusus; on both occasions their grandfather gave largess,[11] probably of 240 sesterces.[12] And the people who received these gifts numbered presumably 200,000 or more.[13] And Dio tells us: " All the money that he bestowed upon people was counted out at once in his sight; for since under Augustus the officials who paid over the money had been wont to deduct large sums for themselves from such donatives, he took good care that this should not happen in his reign." [14]

Velleius again writes: " How gladly, whenever he could do so with the senate's sanction, did he raise to the required rating the fortunes of senators, but in such a way as not to encourage extravagant living, nor yet to allow senators to lose their rank because of honest poverty! " [15] Tacitus enables us to particularize. In A. D. 15 Tiberius heard the petition of Propertius Celer to withdraw from the senatorial order on account of his poverty. Tiberius, learning that the financial embarrassment was inherited from Celer's father, not due to the extravagance or other fault of Celer himself, presented him with a million sesterces, the full amount of the senatorial census. To certain other senators this evidently looked like a good thing; others tried the same

---

[10] Tac., 2. 42. 1.
[11] Id., 3. 29. 3; 4. 4. 1; Suet., 54. 1.
[12] Dio, 59. 2. 2.
[13] Id., 55. 10. 1.
[14] Id., 57. 10. 4 (Loeb).
[15] Vell., 2. 129. 3 (Loeb); cf. Dio, 57. 10. 3.

device. Tiberius ordered them to show the Senate good cause why they should receive such assistance.[16] And so, says Suetonius, who like Seneca is not very enthusiastic or approving, " diffidence and a sense of shame kept many from applying, among them Hortalus, grandson of Quintus Hortensius the orator." [17] But the next year the question arose again, and Tiberius made a pronouncement of policy. The episode is interesting and instructive, and, incidentally, apposite today; we may quote Tacitus' account of it. " And he aided the financial status of certain senators. It was therefore the more remarkable that he received so rudely the petition of the young noble, Marcus Hortalus, in his obvious poverty [Suetonius said he was deterred by shame from applying]. He was the grandson of the orator Hortensius, induced by a grant of a million sesterces from the deified Augustus to marry and raise a family, so that his famous house should not become extinct. While his four children stood at the door of the Curia, when his turn came to voice his opinion, he spoke as follows: ' Senators, these children whose number and youth you see, I raised not of my own will [nice, fond father] but because the Emperor enjoined it; also my ancestors had earned the right to posterity. For I, who in the vicissitudes of the times had not been able to inherit or acquire money nor popularity nor eloquence, that common birthright of our house, was satisfied if my meagre means were neither disgrace to me nor burden to anyone else. Bidden by the Emperor, I married [the lady must

---

[16] Tac., 1. 75. 5-7.
[17] Suet., 47 (Loeb). Cf. the story told by Seneca, *Ep.*, 122. 10: when Acilius Buta, having wasted a huge estate, confessed his bankruptcy to Tiberius, the latter commented " Sero experrectus es."

have felt complimented] and here before you are the stock and offspring of so many consuls, so many dictators [in the line were one dictator, one consul and one consul-designate]. I recount this not to stir odium, but to win compassion. They will attain, Caesar, in your happy reign what honors you will grant; until then protect from want the great-grandsons of Quintus Hortensius, the fosterlings of the deified Augustus! '

" The Senate's inclination to approve prompted Tiberius the more to opposition, in this vein: ' If everyone who is poor comes here and begins to beg money for his children, individuals will never be satisfied and the State will be bankrupted. And our ancestors did not grant the right to go outside the subject of the motion and to present in lieu of opinion something conducing to the common interest, so that we should here promote private concerns and personal fortunes while bringing odium on the Senate and the leaders equally whether they give or refuse their bounty. For this is not a petition, it is a demand, unseasonable and unforeseen, when the senators are convened to debate other matters, to rise and by a statement of the number and ages of one's children to put pressure on the reserve of the Senate, to transfer the same coercion to me and, as it were, to force entrance into the treasury, which, if we empty it by favoritism, must be filled by crimes. The deified Augustus gave you money, Hortalus, but not because he had to, nor with the understanding that he would continue always to give it. Otherwise industry will languish, indolence thrive, if a man fears or hopes nothing from himself, and all men without a care in the world will wait for outside relief, worthless to themselves, a burden to us.' These words and more like them, though heard with approval by those whose habit it is to praise all actions of the Emperor honorable or dishonorable [which seems rather to put me in my place] were by the majority received with silence or a suppressed murmur. Tiberius sensed the feeling; and after a short pause, he said he had given Hortalus his answer, but if the Senate so voted, he would give each of his male children two hundred thousand sesterces. Others expressed thanks; Hortalus remained silent, whether from fear or even in the straits of fortune retaining something of his ancestral nobility [Tiberius gave the better explanation than the historian—odium equally whether the bounty is given or withheld]. Nor did Tiberius thereafter show charity again, although the Hortensian house sank into ignominious poverty." [18] Here, it would seem, is an answer not without much justification to Seneca's censure of the manner of Tiberius' giving to Marius Nepos.

We know also of cases of generosity under various circumstances to other individuals. There is the general statement of Dio [19] that he contributed large sums to individuals (as well as cities) and would accept no honor or laudation for such acts, and that he would not accept legacies from testators who left surviving relatives. But detail of persons and circumstances is more interesting. We may assume that a large part of Sejanus' fortune was given him by Tiberius, since after its confiscation to the *aerarium* it was transferred to the fiscus under a *senatusconsultum* moved by senators who must

---

[18] Tac., 2. 37, 38.   [19] 57. 17. 8.

surely have acted at Tiberius' suggestion.[20] The house
of his nephew, the future Emperor Claudius, was destroyed by fire, and the Senate voted to restore it at
state expense; but Tiberius vetoed the decree and promised to make the loss good of his own *liberalitas*.[21]
Aurelius Pius petitioned aid of the Senate alleging his
house had been weakened by the building of a street
and an aqueduct; the praetors of the treasury opposed
the request and Tiberius gave Aurelius the value of his
house; Tacitus comments: " He was eager to spend
money for honorable purposes—a virtue which he long
retained, even when he abandoned all others." [22] That
was in A. D. 15. Two years later Aemilia Musa died
intestate and her property was claimed by the treasury;
but Tiberius, learning the connection of the deceased
with Marcus Aemilius Lepidus, awarded the estate to
him. Tacitus continues: " et Pantulei, divitis equitis
Romani, hereditatem, quamquam ipse heres in parte
legeretur, tradidit M. Servilio, quem prioribus neque
suspectis tabulis scriptum compererat." [23] A passage of
Pliny,[24] referring by implication to Domitian, enables
us to interpret this incident. It is clear that someone,
determined to inherit from Pantuleius, had forged a will
naming himself as heir together with Tiberius, believing
evidently that acceptance of the forgery would be
assured by the Emperor's interest in it. The genuine-
ness of the new will was, however, called into question—
this is clearly implied in " prioribus neque susceptis
tabulis "—and Tiberius intervened to disallow the

[20] Tac., 6. 2. 1; cf. 4. 20. 1.   [23] *Id.*, 2. 48. 1.
[21] Suet., *Claud.*, 6. 2.   [24] *Pan.*, 43. 1.
[22] Tac., 1. 75. 4.

forged will and execute the earlier and valid will.[25] The nobility of Lepidus and Servilius, said the Emperor, should receive this financial assistance, and Tacitus praises his " grata liberalitas." [26] After the death of Germanicus, Clutorius Priscus composed a poem in his honor and was rewarded by an honorarium from Tiberius.[27] In A. D. 19 it became necessary to appoint a successor to Occia who had served fifty-seven years as a Vestal Virgin. Fonteius Agrippa and Domitius Pollio won the Emperor's thanks by the rivalry with which they offered their daughters. Pollio's daughter was preferred because Agrippa had divorced his wife. But the disappointed candidate Tiberius consoled with a dowry of a million sesterces.[28] The next year Marcus Piso preceded his father home from Syria to the capital bearing messages designed to mollify Tiberius' attitude toward the elder Piso's administration of his province. The Emperor received the young man affably and gave him an honorarium with that *liberalitas* which was customary toward the sons of noble families.[29] The same year Aemilia Lepida was convicted at least of forgery, if not also of adultery and attempted murder, and the senatorial court ordered the confiscation of her property. But Lepida had once been the wife of Aemilius Scaurus who had a daughter by her; and as a concession to him Tiberius waived the confiscation, the property going presumably to Scaurus' daughter.[30] In A. D. 23 with the motive of increasing the dignity of

---

[25] Cf. F. M. Wood, " Domitian and the Roman People: *Fides Publica*," shortly to be published.

[26] Tac., *loc. cit.*

[27] Tac., 3. 49. 1.

[28] *Id.*, 2. 86.

[29] *Id.*, 3. 8. 2.

[30] *Id.*, 3. 23. 3.

the priesthoods and inducing greater willingness to enter the service of the state religion, a *senatusconsultum*, which seems clearly to have been prompted by Tiberius, settled two million sesterces on a newly appointed Vestal Virgin, Cornelia.[31] About the same year, according to Dio, an architect received a grant of money for his achievement in restoring to its vertical position a leaning portico.[32] The composition of a dialogue in which a mushroom, a fig-picker, an oyster and a thrush (or was it a sea-carp?) were characters, won for Asellius Sabinus an honorarium of two hundred thousand sesterces.[33] And we know that under the terms of Tiberius' will legacies were left to many persons (" plerisque ") including the Vestal Virgins;[34] one other beneficiary can be identified—his nephew Claudius, again, received about two million sesterces.[35]

Very many persons must have had aid from the operations of the " Reconstruction Finance Corporation " in A. D. 33. In a period of contracting currency, interest rates had risen above the legal maximum and debtors had borrowed more than they could repay. Now charges were brought of the violation of the legal interest rate and so numerous were the defendants that the problem was referred to the Senate and the Emperor, who granted eighteen months' time to adjust matters in accordance with the law. Loans were called and money became very scarce. The Senate then ordered creditors to invest two thirds of their funds in Italian land; that aggravated the situation by hurrying

[31] *Id.*, 4. 16. 6.
[32] Dio, 57. 21. 6.
[33] Suet., 42. 2.

[34] *Id.*, 76.
[35] *Id.*, *Claud.*, 6. 2.

the calling of loans, depreciating real estate values, and delaying reinvestment by offering hope of bigger bargains to come as the price of land fell. Finally the shortage of money and credit was successfully met by the Emperor who set up a banking commission to lend, on double security in land, one hundred million sesterces without interest for three years.[36]

Aid was extended to the populace of Rome on several occasions when fire caused disastrous losses. Velleius writes: " With what generosity at the time of the recent fire on the Caelian Hill, as well as on other occasions, did he use his private fortune to make good the losses of people of all ranks in life! " [37] Of the other occasions referred to, Dio preserves record of one in A. D. 16; in that year Tiberius, and Livia too, gave assistance to the sufferers from conflagrations.[38] The fire on the Caelian occurred in 27, and Tacitus and Suetonius give some detail, which Velleius' brevity does not allow. The disaster followed close upon the collapse of the speculative amphitheatre at Fidenae. The populace muttered that the year was certainly ill-fated, the Emperor should not have gone to Capreae to live, omens were bad. Hoi polloi, says Tacitus, always blame chance events on somebody. But Tiberius paid over money to the victims in proportion to their losses; and seemingly that ended the muttering, reversed the omens and made the retirement to Capreae acceptable and proper. For the Senate passed a vote of thanks and the populace gave voice to

[36] Tac., 6. 16 f.; Suet., 48. 1; Dio, 58. 21. 5. Cf. K. Scott and R. S. Rogers in *The Clevelander*, 6 (1931/32), # 10, pp. 7 and 18; for a different view see Frank in *A. J. P.*, 56 (1935), 336-341.

[37] Vell., 2. 130. 2 (Loeb).

[38] Dio, 57. 16. 2.

its gratitude, because " he had aided with his liberality even persons unknown and actually encouraged to apply." There were motions also in the Senate to re-name the hill Augustus, because a statue of Tiberius in the house of a senator escaped the flames while all around it was consumed.[39] Suetonius says Tiberius ordered the renaming;[40] and Platner and Ashby remark: " There is no record of the use of the name, and it probably did not survive after the death of Tiberius even in official documents."[41] Is this not a case of " how the story grew "? Tacitus does not state that the motions were passed into a decree; and we shall see that Tiberius had no use for adulation.[42] In their accounts of this episode Velleius uses the word *liberalitas,* Suetonius *munificentia* and Tacitus *munificentia* and *largitio.* The year before Tiberius' death another conflagration destroyed part of the circus adjoining the Aventine and the buildings on the hill itself. Tiberius set up a commission whose members were his four grandsons-in-law with the addition of one nominee of the consuls, this commission to assess the loss sustained by each owner of house or apartment building. The sum set at the commission's disposal to reimburse property-owners was again one hundred million sesterces, and this *munificentia* redounded to his glory. Tacitus concludes: " In accord with the ingenuity of each individual honors were invented and voted to the Emperor. What he rejected or accepted remained unknown, since the end of his life was near."[43] We may recall the

---

[39] Tac., 4. 64.
[40] Suet., 48. 1.
[41] Platner-Ashby, *Topogr. Dict.,* 62.

[42] *Infra,* 85 f.
[43] Tac., 6. 45. 1-4; cf. Dio, 58. 26. 5.

historian's comment in the matter of Aurelius Pius' house twenty one years before that Tiberius was ready and eager to spend, given a good cause—" a virtue which he long retained," [44] and remark the under-statement. Tiberius in his will left forty five million sesterces τῷ δήμῳ.[45]

" The munificence of the emperor claims for its province the losses inflicted by fortune not merely on private citizens, but on whole cities," writes Velleius.[46] In A. D. 17 Asia Minor was shaken by a destructive earthquake, the worst in men's memory. Sardes suffered most severely, and Tiberius extended ten million sesterces to its relief, together with remission of all taxes for the ensuing five years. Magnesia by Mt. Sipylus sustained less loss and received less aid, but seemingly the same remission of taxes. Six other Lydian cities, Philadelphia, Apollonis, Mostene, Hyrcania, Hierocaesarea and Tmolus, and four in Aeolis, Temnos, Aegeae, Myrina and Cyme were exempted from taxes for the same period and an ex-praetor was dispatched by the Senate, doubtless on Tiberius' motion, to investigate and care for immediate needs.[47] Tacitus styles this a " magnifica largitio." [48] Six years later Cibyra in Phrygia and Aegium in the Peloponnese were destroyed from the same cause and on Tiberius' motion the Senate

[44] *Supra*, 10.
[45] Dio, 59. 2. 2; cf. Suet., 76. It is uncertain whether τῷ δήμῳ means the populace or the state treasury; cf. the sources on the similar bequest of Augustus, Tac., 1. 8. 3; Suet., *Aug.*, 101. 2; Dio, 57. 14. 2, and Furneaux and Nipperdey *ad Tac.*, *loc. cit.*
[46] 2. 126. 4 (Loeb); cf. Dio, 57. 10. 3.
[47] Tac., 2. 47; Dio, 57. 17. 7; Strabo, 12. 8. 18; 13. 3. 5; 13. 4. 8; Pliny, *N. H.*, 2. 200; *B. M. C.*, Tib., # 70-73; and on Sardes also *Anth. Pal.*, 9. 423.
[48] Tac., 2. 48. 1.

granted them remission of three years' tribute.[49] And again, evidently in A. D. 29, Ephesus had the same misfortune, but we possess no details of what was done for it.[50]

The Asiatic cities expressed their gratitude repeatedly and enduringly. Mostene and Aegeae, at least, made dedications, respectively in Greek and Latin, to Tiberius as the " founder of twelve cities at one time ";[51] and the fact that the formula is identical in the two inscriptions suggests that other cities may have taken the same action. After the destruction of Cibyra in A. D. 23, we know that representatives of the thirteen cities met at Sardes and passed some resolution [52] whose specific provisions are not preserved. But five of the cities to our knowledge, took the name Caesarea in Tiberius' honor: Hierocaesarea now began to be so-called, instead of Hierakome;[53] Mostene, Sardes, Cyme and Cibyra added the name on their coins;[54] and it appears sometimes also in inscriptions.[55] Cibyra also initiated a new era of the city.[56] Finally, in A. D. 30 all fourteen cities joined together in the dedication of a colossus of Tiberius in Rome beside the temple of Venus, with allegorical

---

[49] *Id.*, 4. 13. 1.

[50] Dess., 156 and commentary.

[51] Dess., 8785 (= *I. G. R. R.*, IV, 1351); *C. I. L.*, III, 7096.

[52] *I. G. R. R.*, IV, 1514. The names remaining on the damaged stone are Mostene, Cibyra, Magnesia, Apollonis, Hierocaesarea, Hyrcania, Myrina and Temnos.

[53] *B. M. C.*, *Lydia*, p. lvii f., and coins, *passim*.

[54] Mostene: *B. M. C.*, *Lydia*, p. lxxv, and coins # 7, 8; Sardes: *op. cit.*, p. cvi f., and coins # 98-101, 110-112; Cyme: *B. M. C.*, *Troas, Aeolis, Lesbos*, coins # 126, 127; Cibyra: *B. M. C.*, *Phrygia*, p. lxvii, and coins *passim*.

[55] *I. G. R. R.*, IV, 900, 1502.

[56] *B. M. C.*, *Phrygia*, p. xlvii.

figures to represent the different cities.[57] Modeled after that monument was one set up in Puteoli by the *Augustales*, whose base now stands in the Naples Museum.[58] But Suetonius was not satisfied; the chapter which records that Tiberius showed *munificentia* to the people only twice—after the fire on the Caelian, and in the financial panic of 33—and how seldom any donatives were given to the troops, concludes: " Not even the provinces benefited from any *liberalitas*, except Asia when the cities were destroyed by earthquake." [59] That is damnation with faint praise indeed.

It is proper to include as *liberalitas* also the public works, as Velleius' *munificentia* shows.[60] Very familiar are the statements of Tacitus, Suetonius and Dio that he left none except the temple of Divus Augustus and the restoration of the theatre of Pompey; [61] and according to Suetonius even those were left unfinished; but Tacitus disagrees, and coins may possibly confirm his version.[62] But that is hardly the whole truth. For, says Dio, he restored all the buildings that had been damaged, completed the buildings which Augustus had begun but not finished, and expended large sums in rebuilding or ornamenting practically all the public works; in every case he declined to inscribe his own name, but left that of the original builder,[63] in accord with an element of his character which we shall later study.[64]

[57] Phlegon of Tralles in Jacoby, *F. G. H.*, II, B, 257, fr. 36, p. 1182.
[58] Dess., 156 (= *C. I. L.*, X, 1624).
[59] Suet., 48. 2.
[60] 2. 130. 1.
[61] Tac., 3. 72. 4; 6. 45. 2; Suet., 47; *Cal.*, 21; Dio, 57. 10. 2.
[62] Tac., *loc. cit.*; cf. Mattingly in *B. M. C.*, I, p. cxxxix.
[63] Dio, *loc. cit.*
[64] *Infra*, 60 ff.

His work in the capital was work of restoration and repair. Yet Velleius writes: " What public buildings did he construct in his own name or that of his family! With what pious munificence, exceeding human belief, does he now rear the temple to his father! With what a magnificent control of personal feeling did he restore the works of Gnaeus Pompey when destroyed by fire! For a feeling of kinship leads him to protect every famous monument." [65] And we hear specifically of some other works belonging to his reign: triumphal arches beside the temple of Mars Ultor in A. D. 18 to commemorate the successes of Germanicus and Drusus in Germany and Illyricum, two other arches of Germanicus,[66] a bridge at the *Naumachia*,[67] paintings for the temple of Augustus, one of which, however, Augustus himself had acquired,[68] and a statue of Apollo for the library of that temple.[69] The statements of Velleius and Dio justify our adding further the temples of Fors Fortuna in Caesar's gardens by the Tiber (A. D. 16),[70] of Liber, Libera and Ceres by the Circus Maximus, of Flora, of Janus in the *forum holitorium*, and of Spes in the next year.[71] Beyond the capital to Italy and the provinces we cannot go. Is a reason for Tiberius' failure to undertake more building to be found (as one of my students suggests) in a reluctance to alter the aspect of Rome from what Augustus had made it? Such change might diminish the fame of his predecessor. There is, at least, an analogy in his own statement of his aim in strictly limiting his own worship so that the cult of Augustus

[65] Vell., 2. 130. 1 (Loeb).
[66] Tac., 2. 64. 2; 2. 41. 1; 2. 83. 3.
[67] Pliny, *N. H.*, 16. 190, 200.
[68] *Op. cit.*, 35. 28, 131.

[69] Suet., 74.
[70] Tac., 2. 41. 1.
[71] *Id.*, 2. 49.

should not be depreciated—"vanescet Augusti honor si promiscis adulationibus vulgatur."[72]

Finally in A.D. 19 when a severe shortage of grain made the Roman populace restive, Tiberius fixed the market price and himself promised to pay the grain merchants a profit of two sesterces per *modius*.[73]

Unhappily for us, in many instances of this *liberalitas* no figures are given, but the total of the sums known may be worth reckoning up. To the soldiers, the donatives at his accession, and to the praetorians after Sejanus' overthrow, with the legacies under his will total well in excess of 5½ million gold dollars, and the very incomplete figures for the populace, the senators and other individuals, and the city of Sardes make up about 13½ million more, not including the loan in the financial panic of 33.

Surely there is in this enough and to spare of justification for Velleius' effusive and exclamatory admiration of Tiberius' *liberalitas*. It would be cause for no wonder if Tiberius had chosen publicly to claim credit for his munificent generosity to fellow-citizens in Rome and his subjects in the provinces. That he did not do. *Liberalitas* does not, so far as I have observed, appear in the inscriptions of the reign; nor is it officially propagandized on the coins (in fact, it does not make its appearance as a coin-legend until Hadrian).[74] But beyond the semi-official Velleius and the more sober factual statements of Tacitus, Dio and Suetonius (and even the last of these we have seen to be very sparing of his praise) Tiberius' benefactions in money went

---

[72] *Id.*, 4. 37. 5.   [73] *Id.*, 2. 87. 1.   [74] *B. M. C.*, I, II, index of legends.

unrecognized, uncommemorated, except by the cities of Asia.

The mention of public works and grain supply leads us to consideration of a second imperial virtue, for the building of works of public utility and the provision of a constant and adequate grain supply were among the manifestations of an Emperor's *providentia*. Charlesworth[75] has defined *providentia*: " that foresight which . . . helped to secure the continued and peaceful existence of the state, preserving it against external and internal dangers "; " the constant care and the almost paternal solicitude that Augustus showed for the welfare of his subjects "; " it manifests itself chiefly in three ways, by caring for the welfare of the people, by providing for a stable succession, and by warding off conspiracies." [76]

Pronouncements of Tiberius on several occasions and in various connections show his awareness of his obligations and his pride in their fulfilment. And the record of his performance may be traced in the historians and its honored recognition in the inscriptions.

In A. D. 22 the aediles set forth to the Senate the need of some action in restraint of the wide-spread extravagance which made a mockery of the sumptuary laws. The Senate referred the matter without prejudice to the Emperor. And Tiberius, temporarily resident in Capreae, communicated his opinions in writing to the Senate. Tacitus[77] records the substance of the letter, from which

[75] M. P. Charlesworth, " Providentia and Aeternitas," in *Harv. Theol. Rev.*, 29 (1936), 107-132. I gratefully acknowledge an obvious and considerable indebtedness in what follows to that essay.

[76] *Loc. cit.*, 108, 109, 110.

[77] 3. 53 f.

we make some excerpts. "I can neither honorably keep silent nor expediently speak out, for I do not sustain the rôle of aedile or praetor or consul. Something larger and loftier is demanded of the *princeps*. . . . How small that matter is of which the aediles advise; if you look at our other problems, how lightly this is to be regarded. But no one asks the Senate to consider that Italy requires imports, that the life of the Roman people is daily exposed to the hazards of sea and storm. And if the resources of the provinces do not come to the aid of master and slave and field, our estates and villas will, I suppose, maintain us! This, Senators, is the burden that the *princeps* sustains; its abandonment will bring the State to ruin."

Three years later when Farther Spain asked, following the precedent set in Asia, to erect a temple for the worship of Tiberius, the Emperor made an official announcement of policy for the future. In the course of that statement he said: "That I am mortal and perform the functions of men, and that I am satisfied if I fulfil the post of *princeps*, I call you, Senators, to witness and I wish posterity to remember, who will grant enough and to spare of credit to my memory, provided they believe me worthy of my forebears, provident of your interests, firm in danger, and unfearful of enmities incurred for the welfare of the State." [78]

Shortly after that incident, Sejanus asked the hand of Livilla in marriage, and Tiberius answered him in part to this effect: " Other mortals can make their plans on the basis of what they think most conducive to their own interests. The lot of a *princeps* is different, who

[78] Tac., 4. 38. 1.

must guide matters of special importance according to public opinion. . . . Therefore I will speak frankly" and he refused the suit.[79]

There occurred in A. D. 32 a serious shortage of grain and the populace was near to insurrection, agitating with more than the usual license against the Emperor. Tiberius, aroused, censured magistrates and Senate for their failure to suppress the disturbance and added a statement " from what provinces and in how much larger quantity than Augustus he was importing a supply of grain." [80]

In his dispatch reporting to the Senate the successful settlement of the revolt of Sacrovir, Tiberius wrote that " fide ac virtute legatos, se consiliis superfuisse," and " added reasons why neither he nor Drusus had gone to the war, exalting the dignity of the Empire and saying it did not become members of the imperial family, if one or two communities were disaffected, to leave the capital which was the center of government for the whole." [81]

These passages show some of the aspects and manifestations of *providentia* and some of the vocabulary descriptive of that virtue. With those in mind let us now survey the activity of Tiberius which called forth tribute to his *providentia*.

The preëminent meaning and mission of the Empire was peace and good order after the war and chaos of a century of civil strife. We should, then, expect to find Tiberius' foresight exercised to maintain peace and order, or when they were disturbed to restore them. Numerous military operations, mostly rather minor,

[79] *Id.*, 4. 40. 1-3.   [80] *Id.*, 6. 13. 1 f.   [81] *Id.*, 3. 47. 1 f.

occurred during the reign, and in other episodes armed
forces were present in case of need, but settlements
were obtained by the show, without the use, of arms.
There were mutinies in Pannonia and Germany, campaigns in Germany, rebellions in Africa, Gaul, Thrace,
Germany and Cappadocia, the threat to the Empire of
Germans warring with each other on its border, two
settlements " short of war," as the phrase now is, with
Parthia.

The mutinies in Pannonia and Germany were put
down by Tiberius' sons, Drusus and Germanicus. But
before Rome knew of the suppression of the former it
heard of the latter's outbreak, and there was in consequence much criticism of Tiberius, the character of
which Tacitus summarizes and the Emperor's answer to
which he gives. People said " the soldiers were disaffected and could not be checked by the unmatured
authority of two youths. He ought to have gone himself
and opposed the Emperor's majesty to the mutineers
who would have yielded when they saw a *princeps* of
long experience and with supreme power to punish or
reward. In the face of all this gossip Tiberius maintained his fixed determination not to leave the capital,
nor hazard himself and the State. . . . In the persons
of his sons he could meet both armies equally, without
impairing his majesty which was more respected at a
distance. Also the youths might excusably refer some
matters to their father, and resistance offered to them
could be moderated or crushed by him; what recourse
was there if the emperor should be scorned? " [82]

When Tiberius withdrew Germanicus from the Ger-

[82] *Id.*, 1. 46 f.

man campaigns, it was with the statement that in his own experience he had accomplished " plura consilio quam vi." [83] Drusus was dispatched to Bohemia to keep watch on the threat of the war between Maroboduus and Arminius as " paci firmator "; [84] and Velleius calls him the " executor and adjutant of Tiberius' *consilia*." [85] The successes of Drusus there and of Germanicus in the settlement of the Armenian question with Parthia were more gratifying to Tiberius, says Tacitus, [86] " because he had maintained peace by diplomacy than if he had won a war by campaigning." The same historian commences his account of the episode of Rhescuporis with the remark, "About nothing was Tiberius so anxious as that orderly arrangements should not be upset," and says that he attacked the problem with cunning (" astu ") . [87] Similarly Velleius exclaims: " With what *prudentia* did he summon Rhescuporis to Rome! " [88] The lexicon allows *prudentia* only rarely the meaning " forethought " or " foresight," giving as the usual definition " prudence, knowledge " and the like. But I wonder whether here *prudentia* has not its cognate's significance. Velleius has earlier written of Tiberius' campaigns under Augustus: " What opportunities to evade the enemy forces did our general's *prudentia* furnish! " and " with what *prudentia* did he dispose our winter quarters! " and has paid tribute to " caelestissima eius opera." [89]

" The African war," writes Velleius, " was soon buried, under his auspices and by his plans." [90] In the

[83] *Id.*, 2. 26. 3.
[84] *Id.*, 2. 46. 6; cf. *infra*, 119 f.
[85] Vell., 2. 129. 3.
[86] 2. 64. 2.

[87] 2. 65. 1; 2. 64. 2.
[88] Vell., 2. 129. 1.
[89] 2. 111. 4; 2. 104. 3.
[90] 2. 129. 4.

relations with Parthia toward the end of his reign Tiberius was "faithful to his determination to manage foreign affairs by policy and cunning without resort to arms," says Tacitus.[91] And of army recruiting Velleius[92] remarks, "quanta cum quiete hominum rem perpetui praecipuique timoris, supplementum, sine trepidatione delectus providet!"

So, too, with disorders in the civil population. Suetonius says Tiberius not only suppressed such commotions when they occurred but guarded assiduously ("sedulo cavit") against their rise.[93] And again Tacitus enables us to particularize. Disorderly conduct of the acting profession in A. D. 14 and 15, which in the latter year reached the point of rioting and bloodshed, was checked by legislative measures.[94] Again in 23 the actors were guilty of insurrection and immoralities, and were expelled from Italy.[95] Inordinate demonstrations of mourning after Germanicus' death, and popular hostility to Piso expressed in violence at his trial were repressed by edicts.[96] An incipient slave revolt near Brundisium in 24 was put down by the military.[97] Agitation in favor of Agrippina and Nero which threatened sedition was suppressed by edict;[98] so, also, riotous protests at the high price of grain in 32.[99]

The administration of the grain supply was to Tiberius, as also to Augustus, one of the Emperor's principal cares for his people, part of his *providentia*. We have already mentioned how he once assured a moderate

[91] 6. 32. 1.
[92] 2. 130. 2.
[93] Suet., 37. 2.
[94] Tac., 1. 54. 3; 1. 77.
[95] *Id.*, 4. 14. 4; Dio, 57. 21. 3.

[96] Tac., 3. 4-6; 3. 14. 5 f.
[97] *Id.*, 4. 27.
[98] *Id.*, 5. 4. 3-5. 1.
[99] *Id.*, 6. 13.

price by himself paying the merchants a margin of profit; his description of that task as the major duty of the *princeps*; his pride in the fact that he imported larger quantities than had Augustus.[100] And Tacitus specifically absolves him of any blame when the populace suffered from shortage, since, says the historian, " he obviated the effects of unfruitful lands or stormy seas so far as expense or care could do." [101]

Similarly the restoration of Asia's cities could be thought of as *providentia*; Strabo [102] so calls it, πρόνοια. And in a passage of Josephus,[103] describing Tiberius' habit of retaining governors long at their posts and containing the Emperor's parable of the sick man plagued with flies, appears the word προμηθεία which seems to mean something like *providentia*; [104] the reference here is to Tiberius' care that the provincials shall not be unnecessarily exposed to the oppressions and exactions of rapacious governors.

But perhaps the most interesting aspect of *providentia* is the preclusion or suppression of conspiracies and the care for the succession.

There were in the course of the reign four conspiracies. One, so to speak relict from Augustus' reign, had had as its original principal Agrippa Postumus; upon his execution at Tiberius' accession one of his slaves, Agrippa Clemens, attempted to impersonate him and head a rebellion. He was captured and put to death; no action was taken against his supporters but the movement appears to have collapsed.[105] In the same year,

[100] *Supra*, 19, 21, 22.
[101] Tac., 4. 6. 6.   [103] *Ant.*, 18. 172.
[102] 13. 4. 8.   [104] Charlesworth, *loc. cit.*, 113.
[105] *Criminal Trials*, 1 f., 21 f.; cf. A. Spengel in *Sitzb. k. b. Akad. z.*

A. D. 16, Marcus Scribonius Drusus Libo, under indictment for high treason, committed suicide in anticipation
of conviction. The official and probably truthful version
of the conspiracy was that he had plotted to murder
Tiberius, Germanicus, Drusus and the leading nobles of
the State.[106] Of greater magnitude and wider implications were the other two which centered respectively
about Agrippina with her two elder sons, and the praetorian prefect Sejanus. To the former we shall recur in
the next lecture.[107] It was in the detection and suppression of Sejanus' conspiracy [108] that Tiberius' contemporaries most fully and vocally recognized his
exercise of *providentia*. Valerius Maximus, following
a denunciation of Sejanus' attempt, writes: " But the
eyes of the Gods were awake, the stars maintained their
power, altars, shrines, and temples were walled about
with present divinity, and nothing which ought to be on
watch to guard the august life and the fatherland,
allowed itself to relax, and most of all the author and
protection of our safety made provision by divine
counsel that his most excellent merits should not fail
with the ruin of the whole world. Therefore peace
abides, the laws obtain and the course of private and
public business continues undisturbed." [109]   Publius
Viriasius Naso, the proconsul of Crete made a dedication at Gortyna " to the *numen* and the *providentia* of
Tiberius Caesar Augustus and of the Senate in com-

Münch., 6 (1903), 5-11; E. Hohl, *Hermes,* 70 (1935), 350-355; A. E. Pappano, *C. P.,* 36 (1941), 30-45.

[106] *Criminal Trials,* 12-20.
[107] *Infra,* 49 ff. Cf. *Criminal Trials,* 98-103.
[108] *Op. cit.,* 110-116.
[109] Val. Max., 9. 11. ext. 4.

memoration of the 15th day before the Kalends of November."[110] (As a proconsul the dedicator must ascribe foresight to the Senate as well as to the Emperor.) At Corinth there was a dedication "for the safety of Tiberius" and the colony erected an altar and instituted a priest of *Providentia Augusta* and *Salus Publica*.[111] At Interamna in A. D. 32 an *Augustalis* made a dedication "to *Salus Perpetua Augusta*, to the *Libertas Publica* of the Roman people, to the *Genius* of the municipality, and to the *Providentia* of Tiberius Caesar Augustus who was born for the perpetuation of the Roman name, on the occasion of the removal of a most dangerous enemy to the Roman people."[112] In the little town of Rignum on the Flaminian Way an *Augustalis*, in payment of a vow for Tiberius' safety and welfare, made a dedication in A. D. 32/33 "principi optumo et iustissimo, conservatori patriae."[113] Italica in Spain issued a coin whose reverse type was an altar inscribed *Providentia Augusti*.[114] And in Rome itself an altar was erected to *Providentia Augusta*.[115] In the years A. D. 34 to 37 the Roman mint issued *asses*, dated by Tiberius' tribunician power, whose reverse type is a rudder and globe.[116] Mattingly calls this type "a simple and effective

---

[110] Dess., 158 (= *C. I. L.*, III, 12036).

[111] *Corinth*, VIII, ii, 15, 110; for the dating cf. A. B. West's commentary *ad locc.*

[112] Dess., 157 (= *C. I. L.*, XI, 4170). Another inscription of Interamna (Dess., 3793), undated, reading "Providentiae Augustae sacr." may be referred with some assurance to the same time and prompting.

[113] Dess., 159 (= *C. I. L.*, XI, 3872).

[114] A. Heiss, *Monnaies Antiques de l'Espagne*, 380; cf. a coin of Illici with an altar inscribed *Sal. Aug.*, *op. cit.*, 277, 279.

[115] *C. I. L.*, VI, 2028, d, 15; 2033, 5; and on the date cf. Charlesworth, *loc. cit.*, 111 n. 9, and 112.

[116] *B. M. C.*, Tib., 104, 117-119, 135 and (in the appendix) 119 bis.

piece of symbolism, suggesting the wise government of the world by the Emperor," [117] which is to say *Providentia*. So Valerius Maximus, again, sees in Tiberius a " caelestis providentia " and calls Augustus and Tiberius " rei publicae divina ocula." [118]

When Augustus adopted Tiberius and designated him as his successor, Velleius says men " conceived a hope for the perpetual security and eternal existence of the Roman Empire. . . . Then there shone again definite assurance to parents for the safety of their children, to husbands for the sanctity of marriage, to property-owners for the safety of their estates, to all men for safety, order, peace, tranquility." [119] That was what provision of orderly succession to the throne meant to the Romans. In the first five years of Tiberius' reign the plan of the succession stood as Augustus had arranged it—Tiberius' adopted son and natural son, Germanicus and Drusus, were the designated heirs, Augustus' preference resting upon the former and his line. But from the death of Germanicus in A. D. 19 the succession to Tiberius became a problem comparable in its complexities almost to the successively changing plans of Augustus himself a half century before; but it has not received proportionate attention and study. We can but outline it here.

[117] *Op. cit.*, I, cxxxviii. Alföldi interprets the globe, and the globe and rudder, generally, as symbols of *Weltherrschaft, Röm. Mitt.*, L (1935), 117 f. But at least in the case of Tiberius, in view of the historical and chronological context, the reference must be more particular.

[118] Val. Max., 1, praef.; 4. 3. 3.

[119] Vell., 2. 103. 4 f. (Loeb, modified). Syme most unkindly remarks (*The Roman Revolution*, 431, n. 2) " These pious prayers were answered almost at once by famine, pestilence and years of warfare, with grave disasters." But our present concern is men's expectation rather than subsequent historical events.

After Germanicus' death his elder sons Nero and Drusus were entrusted by Tiberius to the care of their uncle Drusus.[120] As each became of age he was dispensed from the minor magistracies and allowed to hold the quaestorship five years before the legal age.[121] Nero married his cousin Julia.[122] Claudius' son Drusus was betrothed to Sejanus' daughter but died before he came of age.[123] Meantime Tiberius' own son Drusus, as heir pending the maturity of Germanicus' children, had held his second consulship, had received for a time an *imperium proconsulare* and then been vested with the tribunician power, only to be murdered by the plotting Sejanus.[124] The young Nero and Drusus were then made wards of the Senate [125] and their names apeared in the *vota* of A.D. 24, though Tiberius vehemently disapproved the latter.[126] It seems to have been intended at that time that Sejanus should be regent in case of Tiberius' death before Nero and Drusus were old enough to rule. A phrase of Velleius, not I think previously noted in this connection, seems to me to contain a hint of this arrangement. Roman history was full of precedents for paying the highest honors to men of merit; so, says Velleius, it was the natural following of a precedent which induced Caesar to make trial of Sejanus and Sejanus to aid the Emperor with his burdens, and brought the Senate and the Roman people willingly to summon the man whom they knew by experience to be best " *in tutelam securitatis suae.*" [127] Sejanus in A.D. 25 asked the hand of Livilla, widow of his recent victim,

[120] Tac., 4. 8. 6.

[121] *Id.*, 3. 29. 1; 4. 4. 1.

[122] *Id.*, 3. 29. 4.

[123] *Id.*, 3. 29. 5; Suet., *Claud.*, 27. 1.

[124] *Infra*, 130 f., 145.

[125] Tac., 4. 8. 7 f.

[126] *Id.*, 4. 17. 1-3.

[127] Vell., 2. 128. 4.

but Tiberius refused; [128] the next year Agrippina, widow
of Germanicus, asked to remarry but Tiberius put her
off without a definite answer.[129] Agrippina, Nero,
Drusus (who having been betrothed to a sister of the
future emperor Otho, had now married an Aemilia
Lepida) [130] and Livilla were subsequently convicted of
conspiracy.[131] But for a time, when Sejanus' conspiracy
threatened success, Drusus was marked to be Tiberius'
heir.[132] Meanwhile Tiberius' four granddaughters, the
younger Agrippina, Drusilla, Julia and the other Julia
(daughter of Drusus and widow of Nero) were married
to Domitius, Cassius, Vinicius and Rubellius respectively; [133] and Gaius, the surviving son of Germanicus,
married Claudilla, the daughter of M. Silanus.[134] As
the reign approached its close, Tiberius' choice was
narrowed to his two grandsons, Gaius and Tiberius
Gemellus, and his nephew Claudius, or else someone
outside the imperial family. The last possibility would
be a dishonor to Augustus; Claudius he considered unfit.
Between Gaius and Gemellus he could not decide; [135]
he is said to have had suspicions of Gaius' loyalty and
doubts of Gemellus' legitimacy; [136] in anxiety over the
choice he consulted Thrasyllus who told him Gaius
would no more rule than he would ride horseback over
the gulf of Baiae.[137] Tiberius died with the decision

[128] Tac., 4. 39 f.
[129] Id., 4. 53.
[130] Suet., Oth., 1. 3; Tac., 6. 40. 4.
[131] Cf. Criminal Trials, 98-103, 106 f., 119-122.
[132] Tac., 6. 23. 5; Suet., 65. 2; Dio, 58. 13. 1.
[133] Tac., 4. 75. 1; 6. 15. 1-4; 6. 27. 1.
[134] Id., 6. 20. 1; Suet., Cal., 12. 1.
[135] Tac., 6. 46. 1-4.
[136] Suet., 62. 3.
[137] Id., Cal., 19. 3.

unmade.[138] What an irony that after all those years of attention, consideration, care,—ample evidence surely of *providentia*,—he should have failed in the end— failed to choose between his grandsons, failed to protect the one against the other, failed to train his eventual successor, as Germanicus and Drusus had been trained, in the service of the State.

Charlesworth has summed up the diverse aspects of *providentia* in the formula: " the *providentia* of the Princeps aims at the *aeternitas* of the Roman people." [139] And he has noted some evidence for the growing associa- tion of the Emperor and the imperial family with the idea of eternity which gathered about the Roman State. We may resume it briefly and make a number of addi- tions. The *princeps* as pontifex maximus was linked with Vesta the eternal goddess; [140] on the anniversary of his election (6 March) and upon the birthdays of Germanicus (24 May), Drusus (7 October), and Ti- berius (16 November) there was ordained a " supplicatio Vestae "; Livia, when she attended the theatre, was privileged to sit with the Vestal Virgins; [141] and we may recall Tiberius' gifts to candidates for the college of Vestals and his legacies to those priestesses.[142] From Augustus' adoption of Tiberius men conceived a " hope of the perpetua securitas aeternitasque imperii Ro- mani." [143] After the overthrow of Sejanus, Tiberius was hailed as " conservator patriae " and " natus ad aeterni- tatem Romani nominis." [144] A similar significance

---

[138] Tac., 6. 46. 5. Josephus, *Ant.*, 18. 205-233, has a story that Tiberius, in obedience to an omen, had designated Gaius.

[139] Charlesworth, *loc. cit.*, 122.   [142] *Supra*, 11 f.

[140] *Ibid.*, 123.   [143] Charlesworth, 123.

[141] *Ibid.*, 124.   [144] *Ibid.*, 124.

underlies the dedicatory offerings to Jupiter after the suppression of Libo's conspiracy.[145] Again when Agrippina, under conviction of conspiracy, died in A. D. 33 on the anniversary of Sejanus' execution, the Senate voted the annual commemoration of 18 October by an offering to Jupiter.[146] With Jupiter were associated on the former occasion Mars and *Concordia*.[147] The mythical founder of the eternal city appears for natural and obvious reasons. That the name of *Concordia* has the self-same implications and symbolism is evident from the association together of *Concordia, Salus Populi Romani* and *Pax* in 10 B. C. in the dedication by Augustus of altars and statues.[148]

Interesting also in this connection is the inscription from Peltuinum which records that two aediles of the town " to the honor of Tiberius Caesar Augustus and his grandsons brought the Aqua Augusta to Peltuinum, *pro aeternitate Caesarum.*" [149] Tiberius himself was aware of the idea, but with becoming modesty deprecated his own share in the symbolism: in the edict by which he endeavored to moderate the excessive mourning for Germanicus he said "principes mortales, rem publicam aeternam esse." [150] Valerius Maximus, again, saw in Tiberius " certissima salus patriae ";[151] and does not this expression suggest a special implication in the phrase " salutaris princeps " which Valerius Maximus

[145] Tac., 2. 32. 4. Cf. Charlesworth, 125.
[146] Tac., 6. 25. 5.
[147] *Id.*, 2. 32. 4; Dess., 153 (= *C. I. L.*, VI, 91); 3782 (= VI, 90); 3783 (= VI, 30856); *C. I. L.*, VI, 92-94.
[148] Dio, 54. 35. 2; Ovid, *Fasti*, 3. 881 f.
[149] Dess., 163 (= *C. I. L.*, IX, 4209).
[150] Tac., 3. 6. 5.
[151] Val. Max., 1, praef.

twice applies to Tiberius? [152] The Emperor himself once employed it, saying in the Senate, " I have said on many other occasions as on this, Senators, that a good and beneficent ruler (*bonus et salutaris princeps*) ought to serve the Senate, and often all the citizens and sometimes individuals too." [153]

Liberalitas and *Providentia*—Tiberius had shown an imperial generosity to his troops, to his fellow-senators, to his fellow-citizens of humbler station, to his subjects in the cities of provinces. By the maintenance of order and the preservation of peace, by their restoration when they were disturbed, by provision of an adequate supply of grain to feed the Roman populace, by the detection and suppression of conspiracies against himself and the State, and by attention to the end to the important problem of insuring the succession, he had shown that he too, not less than his predecessor, possessed that *providentia*, that fatherly care for his people, which the good ruler must manifest or fail of being a good ruler.

[152] *Id.*, 2. 9. 6; 8. 13. praef.
[153] Suet., 29.

II. *CLEMENTIA*

In the Raleigh lecture on History for 1937, Charlesworth discussed " The Virtues of a Roman Emperor: Propaganda and the Creation of Belief." [1] I commend it to your reading as an illuminating and stimulating treatment of the general aspect of Roman Imperial history from Augustus to Constantine, of which a very circumscribed part we are engaged in studying. Part of one paragraph in that lecture provides the starting point for our present essay.

Said Charlesworth: " *Clementia* . . . had been a virtue of Julius Caesar, it was a virtue of Augustus, yet it does not appear on the coins of his successors till Vitellius, and is never pictured on coins of the Flavian dynasty or of Nerva and Trajan. Perhaps that was because its history after Augustus was curious: in A. D. 22 [*lege* 28] Tiberius was voted an *ara Clementiae*; when in 39 Caligula ranted against the Senators as traitors they meekly replied by praising him for his Clemency; Seneca's treatise on Clemency was addressed to Nero. Tiberius, Caligula, Nero, and Vitellius—the list has an ominous ring. . . . In fact, *Clementia* had become too much a despotic quality; the mercy of a conqueror towards those whose life he holds in his hands, the gracious act of an absolute monarch towards his subjects. Possessing that grim significance it was wisely laid aside for a time until its unhappy memories, its ring of civil war or despotism, could be forgotten, and it could return again

[1] M. P. Charlesworth, " The Virtues of a Roman Emperor: Propaganda and the Creation of Belief," *Proc. Brit. Acad.*, 23 (1937), 105-133.

under Hadrian or under later emperors in an altered form as *Clementia Temporum*, 'the mildness of the times.' "[2]

I must demur at the idea that the name of Tiberius gives any list " an ominous ring." But of Tiberius more anon. Let us start at the other end of the list. I hold no brief for Vitellius, but even the devil deserves his due. Charlesworth is not the first to damn the clemency of Vitellius as historically unjustified: Mommsen, with heavy sarcasm, denounced the celebration on coins of Tiberius' and Vitellius' *clementia* and of Vespasian as the "vindicator of the people's liberty," and by inference denied the validity of numismatic evidence.[3] But the coins of Vitellius bearing the legends of *Clementia* and *Aequitas* refer very specifically to the indulgence he had shown to the family of Otho.[4] And Tacitus, certainly no adulator of Vitellius, records that fact and comments "victor clementiae gloriam tulit."[5] By that one act of mercy, quite regardless of all his other acts as Emperor, good, bad, or indifferent, Vitellius lays just and undeniable claim to the possession of the virtue of *clementia*. Nor is it difficult to find numerous occasions on which Nero showed clemency. But, as with Vitellius, let us content ourselves at present with one incident. In A. D. 59 after the necessary and perhaps justifiable, if hardly laudable, removal of his mother Agrippina, " in order to intensify the odium of his mother and to show that his own clemency [*lenitas*] was augmented

---

[2] *Loc. cit.*, 10 f.
[3] Mommsen, *Ges. Schr.*, IV, 352. I owe this reference to O. Th. Schulz, *Die Rechtstitel und Regierungsprogramme auf römischen Kaisermünzen*, 90.
[4] Schulz, *op. cit.*, 91.
[5] Tac., *Hist.*, 1. 75.

by her removal, Nero restored to their homes the distinguished ladies Junia and Calpurnia, and the ex-
praetors Valerius Capito and Licinius Gabolus, whom
Agrippina had banished. He also allowed the ashes of
Lollia Paulina to be brought home and a tomb to be
constructed for them. And Iturius and Calvisius, whom
he had himself lately banished, he now pardoned." [6] Nor
can I quite accept even the aspersions on Gaius. Moved
by a belated feeling of loyalty to his predecessor and
an investigation of the records of the criminal trials, he
denounced the senators as far more responsible than
Tiberius for trials, convictions and executions. More
significant, he asserted that while he might himself
legitimately criticize a previous Emperor, the senators
might not legitimately do the same—criticism of their
former ruler was *maiestas*. And with that he left the
senate-house.[7] If then, having declared that the senators are guilty of *maiestas*,—and the position is certainly
not without much justification—Gaius declines to prose-
cute the charge, that is clemency and the Senators
may rightly feel and express gratitude that he has
spared them.

As regards the criticism that the *clementia* shown by
these emperors was " the mercy of a conqueror towards
those whose life he holds in his hands, the gracious act
of an absolute monarch towards his subjects," I would
answer that there *is* no clemency unless the person who
shows it *has* the power, by withholding his mercy, to
inflict death or other ill. The clemency of both Julius
Caesar and Augustus had been exactly that—" the

[6] Tac., 14. 12. 5 f.   [7] Dio, 59. 16.

mercy of a conqueror towards those whose life he holds in his hands." [7a]

Charlesworth's statement that *Clementia* does not appear on coins between Augustus and Vitellius was taken up by Sutherland.[8] Quoting more briefly the passage from which we took our departure, Sutherland wrote: " This is a challenging paragraph, so written that either emphasis on, or complete neglect of, Clementia in the post-Augustan period may become, equally, evidence of a despotic régime, the particular interpretation depending, in each instance, on more general evidence, to which the historian's reaction may, in fact, vary. But, in any case, Mr. Charlesworth's sketch of Clementia is incomplete, for (and this is his omission) Clementia *does* appear on the coinage of Tiberius, and is accompanied by the kindred Virtue, Moderatio." [9] Sutherland then proceeds to describe and discuss the coin series of Tiberius which present as their reverse types busts of Tiberius full face on ornamented shields or medallions with the legends respectively " Clementiae—S. C." and " Moderationi—S. C." [10] On detailed and technical numismatic evidence he concludes convincingly that there were no emissions between A. D. 22/23 and 34/35, and that all coins dated IMP. VIII or TR. P. XXIIII were probably issued in 22/23.[11] Accepting the suggestion made many years ago by

---

[7a] Not inapposite is a phrase of Seneca: " nisi post crimen supervacua est [clementia] et sola haec virtus inter innocentes cessat," *de Clem.*, 1. 2. 1.

[8] C. H. V. Sutherland, " Two ' Virtues ' of Tiberius: a Numismatic Contribution to the History of his Reign," *J. R. S.*, 28 (1938), 129-140.

[9] Sutherland, *loc. cit.*, 129.

[10] *B. M. C.*, Tib., #85-90.

[11] Sutherland, *loc. cit.*, 129-137.

Mowat [12] that Tiberius was honored with shields of Moderation and Clemency like the famous one dedicated to Augustus, he asks " is it possible to find, in the history of those years, anything which would explain the conferment of such shields on Tiberius, and which would have resulted in these commemorative *dupondii?* " On the evidence that (1) there was no actual conviction for treason until that of Antistius Vetus in A. D. 21 for his intrigue with the King of Thrace; (2) that in the same year Tiberius censured the Senate's precipitate execution of Clutorius Priscus for having written a poetic eulogy of Drusus before Drusus died, and introduced a stay of execution to be observed in the future; and (3) that Tacitus writing of the year 22 says " Tiberius, having obtained a reputation for moderation, because he had checked the rise of the accusers, etc.," Sutherland proposes the hypothesis " that the Senate, in A. D. 22, presented Tiberius with shields of Clemency and Moderation—an act of which an echo is preserved in the pages of Tacitus—and that, the formal but well-earned honor once conferred, the Senate proceeded by means of their coinage to call wide public attention to the imperial virtues which their ceremonial action had just recognized." [13] Shortly he adds: " Six years later, if he was still alive, the mint-master of A. D. 22 had cause for sardonic laughter: Sejanus was then in the saddle, and Tiberius himself at Capreae. The continuation of the Clemency and Moderation of A. D. 22 would then have seemed less certain: perhaps the events of the time had even begun to sug-

[12] *Rev. Num.*, ser. 4, 15 (1911), 338 ff.
[13] Sutherland, *loc. cit.*, 138 f.

gest a *need* for Clementia rather than its celebration. Is this the explanation of the *ara Clementiae* of A. D. 28—a deliberate reminiscence of a conspicuous coin type issued six years before? " [14] And finally: " The ' Clementia ' and ' Moderatio ' *dupondii* are to be regarded as first-hand evidence of the high standard of imperial justice up to the year of issue, A. D. 22/23,—a truth which may be corroborated by modern analysis of the secondary and later evidence of the Annals." [15]

We may now pose several questions:

(1)   Why does Sutherland so readily assume the absence, and the need, of clemency in A. D. 28?

(2)   Are *Clementia* and *Moderatio* the same?

(3)   What constitutes clemency?

(4)   Did Tiberius possess that virtue?

(5)   If so, did he possess it for the first decade of his reign merely, and having then lost it fail to regain it in the remaining thirteen years of his reign?

(6)   Why was an altar of Clemency erected in A. D. 28?

The first question, of course, I cannot really answer; Sutherland himself would have to speak for himself. But I wish to make some relevant comments. The basis on which Sutherland credits Tiberius with clemency in the earlier years seems to be: the absence of trials for treason, or, if there are trials, then the failure of conviction. Now in the year 28 our sources record *one* trial for treason, that of Titius Sabinus which resulted in conviction. The case was brought in the preceding year: the trial, in fact, belonged almost entirely in 27.

[14] *Loc. cit.*, 139 f.   [15] *Loc. cit.*, 140.

For it was concluded on 1 January 28 and Sabinus was executed that day.[16] Is the conviction and execution of Sabinus the reason why clemency is missing and needed in 28? But Sutherland allowed Tiberius the conviction of Antistius in 21 for treason without denying him possession of *clementia*. And does that first day of the year spoil the whole year? Should not the absence of trials for treason in the remaining 364 days establish, by Sutherland's standards, the presence, rather than the absence, of *clementia*? But Sejanus " was in the saddle ": that appears to vitiate the whole record, but why or how, precisely, is not clear.

Clementia and *Moderatio* Sutherland calls kindred virtues;[17] but he does not differentiate them and associates both together with the trials for treason. But the question of their identity or kinship or diversity let us defer to the next lecture.

It seems desirable to have some definition of what constitutes clemency. Sutherland writes: " we think most naturally . . . of the *Lex Iuli* [sic] *maiestatis*," and catalogues charges waived, years without charges of treason, a few convictions, some acquittals and some cases of treason and extortion in which conviction was on the latter charge.[18] But acquittals should have here no place; to adjudge a defendant innocent is not clemency; clemency in the courts presupposes guilt. And again, there is in Sutherland's list the perennial failure to differentiate between that *maiestas* which is high treason—even the jurists often used *maiestas* instead

[16] Tac., 4. 68-70.
[17] Sutherland, *loc. cit.*, 129.
[18] Sutherland, *loc. cit.*, 138 f.

of the more correct *perduellio*—and that which is *lèse majesté*.[19] And finally, of the three years which Sutherland finds free of such charges, two contained trials for high treason, 16 the case of Libo for conspiracy, and 18 that of Rhescuporis, King of Thrace.[20] But why should we think only of trials?

As commander-in-chief of the army the Emperor may, it seems to me, claim credit for that clemency shown by Roman armies to foreign enemies. If the Emperor is offended or injured and takes no action against the offending person, that is clemency. If charges are brought against some person and the Emperor quashes the indictment without trial, that may reasonably be considered clemency—the defendant if tried might have been found guilty and punished. (Here are the " waived charges " of Sutherland). If a trial results in conviction and the Emperor interposes his veto, that is clemency; or if the law provides a more severe penalty and the Emperor intervenes to impose a less severe punishment, that, too, is clemency.

To our fourth question—did Tiberius possess *clementia?*—we answer not, with Sutherland, " yes, but not beyond A. D. 23," rather an unequivocal yes on evidence to appear in the discussion of the next question—Does manifestation of clemency by Tiberius appear after the final date at which Sutherland will admit it? And, incidentally, how much evidence is there really for Tiberius' clemency?

Bearing in mind, then, the definitions of *clementia* set up a moment ago, let us survey Tiberius' reign.

Germanicus promised to Segestes that no harm should

---

[19] *Criminal Trials*, 6 f. [20] Tac., 2. 27-32; 2. 67. 3-5.

come to his children or retainers and that he himself
should have settlement in Roman territory—" clementi
responso " according to Tacitus—and the promise was
redeemed.[21] Flavus, the Romanized German, speaking
for Germanicus, assured Arminius, if he would surrender, of " paratam clementiam " for himself, his wife
and his son; but the offer was rejected.[22] The German
tribe of Angrivarii upon surrender to Stertinius received
a full pardon for all past actions.[23] Maroboduus, fallen
from power and deserted by his subjects, had no recourse but to seek an asylum in Roman territory.
" Misericordia Caesaris " allowed him residence at
Ravenna.[24] Catualda, who had overthrown him, shortly
fell in his turn, and likewise petitioned Roman protection. Again the Emperor's clemency was granted and
Catualda found harbor at Frejus.[25] In the course of the
revolt of Tacfarinas in Africa, impunity was offered by
Junius Blaesus to those rebels who would surrender, and
many deserted their leader to take advantage of that
offer.[26] And in the Thracian revolt one leader who
counselled surrender and himself acted upon that
counsel was motivated, according to Tacitus, by long
experience of Roman power and Roman clemency.[27]
The years to which we have referred are 15, 16, 18, 22
and 26.

Quintus Haterius, having given Tiberius offense, came
to implore pardon and embraced the Emperor's knees.
By accident or impeded by the suppliant, Tiberius fell,
and the guard, suspecting assault, almost put Haterius

---

[21] *Id.*, 1. 58. 8.
[22] *Id.*, 2. 10. 1.
[23] *Id.*, 2. 22. 3.
[24] *Id.*, 2. 63. 1, 5.

[25] *Id.*, 2. 63. 6.
[26] *Id.*, 3. 73. 4 f.
[27] *Id.*, 4. 50. 2.

to death. Not until he had won Livia's intercession, did Haterius receive clemency from Tiberius.[28] The abortive rebellion headed by Agrippa Clemens was alleged to have received financial aid and advice from numerous senators, knights and members of the imperial household; no action was taken however to identify and punish them.[29] Following Tiberius' accession Livia wrote a letter to King Archelaus of Cappadocia frankly informing him of Tiberius' displeasure with him, but holding out a promise of clemency if he would come to Rome to beg it.[30] You will recall Tiberius' grant of eighteen months' time in which senatorial creditors might arrange their financial affairs in accord with the laws which they had been violating.[31] And there is the positive statement by Suetonius, borne out by verbatim quotation from Tiberius, that he refused to take any repressive action against libel and slander of himself.[32] Dio corroborates with two stories: A praetor was accused of slander or some such offense against the Emperor; he left the Senate, took off his magisterial robes and returning demanded that indictment be lodged against him immediately; at which, says Dio, Tiberius was grieved and did not molest him.[33] The same historian narrates that Lucius Caesianus in his praetorship arranged that at the Floralia all the merrymaking until nightfall was done by baldheads, and after dark provided light by torches in the hands of 5000 boys with

[28] Id., 1.13. 4-7.
[29] Id., 2. 40. 6.
[30] Id., 2. 42. 4.

[31] Id., 6.16. 5.
[32] Suet., 28.
[33] Dio, 57. 21. 2.

shaven heads—all this to make fun of the bald Tiberius,
who pretended he hadn't heard about it.[34] All this, too,
is clemency; the years are 14, 16, 22, 32, and 33.

Charges of *maiestas* in A. D. 15 against two knights,
Faianius and Rubrius, and a senator, Granius Marcellus, were quashed by Tiberius, and in 17 likewise in the
case of Appuleia Varilla.[35] Three years later he refused
trial of the same charge against Aemilia Lepida, and the
next year against the praetor Caecilianus.[36] In 22 the
charge of *maiestas* against Gaius Silanus seems to have
been quashed, as also that against Caesius Cordus,
and it is certain that indictment of a knight, Lucius
Ennius was refused.[37] Two years later indictments of
Lucius Piso for *vis publica* and of Gnaeus Lentulus and
Lucius Tubero for conspiracy, were rejected, and the
next year trial of some unknown charge against Sextus
Marius was denied.[38] In A. D. 31 accusation of *maiestas*
brought against Lucius Arruntius was quashed, as was
also a similar charge the next year against Cotta Messalinus.[39] In 32 also, indictments probably for high
treason against Calvisius Sabinus and Gaius Appius
Silanus were quashed.[40] And in 36 Marcus Julius
Agrippa I appeared before Tiberius at Capreae to accuse
his grandfather Herod Antipas, the tetrarch of Galilee.
It seems probable that the charges were intrigue with

[34] *Id.*, 58. 19. 1 f.
[35] Tac., 1. 73 f.; 2. 50. 4.
[36] *Id.*, 3. 22. 4; 3. 37. 1; cf. *Criminal Trials*, 61.
[37] Tac., 3. 66 ff.; cf. *Criminal Trials*, 67 f.; Tac., 3. 70. 1; cf. 3. 38. 1 and
Criminal Trials, 70; Tac., 3. 70. 2.
[38] *Id.*, 4. 21. 4; 4. 29. 1; 4. 36. 1.
[39] *Id.*, 6. 5-7; cf. *C. P.*, 26 (1931), 37-41; *Hermes*, 68 (1933), 121-123.
[40] Tac., 6. 9. 6.

Sejanus and traffic with King Artabanus of Parthia. Tiberius refused to admit the charges to trial.[41]

Drusus Libo on trial for high treason took his life in anticipation of conviction; Tiberius said upon oath in the Senate that however guilty the defendant might have been, he would have asked the court to grant him life, if he had not committed suicide.[42] I see no reason for refusing to credit that intention. Astrologers were banished from Italy, but some of them obtained clemency on promising to desist from the practice of their art.[43] Appuleia Varilla was convicted of adultery; the Julian law provided relegation to an island, confiscation of half her dowry and one third of her property; this penalty Tiberius deprecated and moved that her family be allowed to banish her two hundred miles from Rome. Her paramour Manlius, instead of relegation to an island and the confiscation of half his property, was forbidden to live in Italy or Africa.[44] When Gnaeus Piso on trial for murder and high treason committed suicide, Tiberius complained of the action, which seems to hint at an intention to move for leniency as in the case of Libo.[45] Conviction followed and the court ordered the confiscation of Piso's property and the condemnation of his memory; Tiberius vetoed both. The court convicted Piso's son Marcus apparently in defiance of the evidence, so Tiberius vetoed that verdict.[46] In Tiberius' first absence to Capreae the Senate convicted Clutorius

[41] Jos., B. J., 2. 178; cf. Criminal Trials, 159 f.
[42] Tac., 2. 31. 4.
[43] Suet., 36.
[44] Tac., 2. 50. 4 f.; Criminal Trials, 28.
[45] Tac., 3. 16. 3.
[46] Id., 3. 18. 1 f.

Priscus of having written an obituary eulogy of Drusus Caesar before Drusus died, and executed him forthwith. Tiberius was furious and ordered that ten days should thereafter intervene between conviction and execution to allow opportunity for exercise of his clemency.[47] Gaius Silanus, convicted of extortion, was sentenced to exile in the island of Gyarus: Tiberius, saying that Gyarus was bleak and uninhabited, substituted Cythnus.[48] When Vibius Serenus was convicted of treason, it was moved to execute him by flogging: Tiberius vetoed the motion; then exile to Gyarus or Donusa was substituted: Tiberius again interposed veto on the ground that neither island had a water supply: and the convict was exiled to Amorgus.[49] Cominius Macer, a Roman knight, was convicted of libellous attack upon Tiberius, but the Emperor pardoned him; Tacitus perversely remarks: " This action made it the more surprising that, cognizant as he was of better things and what good reputation attended clemency, he yet preferred the darker course." [50] When Firmius Catus was convicted of *calumnia*, Tiberius deprecated the sentence of exile, but allowed his expulsion from the Senate.[51] Pomponius Labeo and his wife Paxaea, under accusation of extortion in his province, both committed suicide; Tiberius complained to the Senate that he had been content with forbidding Labeo the palace and his friendship, that the suicide was a cloak for guilt to cast odium upon the Emperor, and that Paxaea, though guilty, would have been pardoned.[52] The dates of these cases are 16, 17, 20, 21, 22, 24 and 34.

[47] *Id.*, 3. 51. 2 f.   [49] *Id.*, 4. 30. 1 f.   [51] *Id.*, 4. 31. 7 f.

[48] *Id.*, 3. 69. 8.   [50] *Id.*, 4. 31. 1 f.   [52] *Id.*, 6. 29. 3.

It will perhaps not be entirely out of place in a discussion of clemency to record that under the Lex Papia Poppaea informers had been so active and so many persons had been ruined that, according to Tacitus, " a reign of terror threatened all," had not Tiberius by setting up a senatorial commission of fifteen to untie some of the legal knots, given for a time some measure of relief.[53] Similarly his refusal to sponsor sumptuary legislation was applauded because it prevented a wave of accusations by informers.[54]

Manius Lepidus, speaking at the trial of Clutorius Priscus, said " I have often heard our *princeps* express regret when some one by taking his own life prevented him from showing clemency."[55] The cases known to us seem to be only two prior to that date, those of Libo and Piso; but it is of course not impossible that there had been others of which our sources are silent. Lucius Piso, before making his motion for sentence upon Gaius Silanus convicted of extortion, spoke at length " de clementia principis."[56] Some unidentified defendant charged with complicity in the conspiracy of Sejanus, announcing his intention of committing suicide, said " I shall not test the cruelty or the clemency of anyone."[57] There was then a clemency which might be tested. If now the hostile critic asserts that the statements of Lepidus and Piso were no more than adulation, I reply that a sufficient number of instances of clemency has been catalogued to justify their words as substantial truth.

[53] *Id.*, 3. 28. 6.
[54] *Id.*, 3. 56. 1; cf. *infra*, 74 f.
[55] Tac., 3. 50. 3.
[56] *Id.*, 3. 68. 2.
[57] *Id.*, 5. 6. 4.

What answer have we then to our fifth question—did Tiberius' clemency end with the first decade of his reign? and how much evidence is there for his possession of that virtue? We have listed very nearly two score examples of clemency of one sort or another. We have found no instances in the years 19, 23, 27 to 30 inclusive, 35 and 37. The four separate years certainly have no significance at all; of the last Tiberius lived only two months and a half. What of the quadrennium 27-30? The year 28 was the date of the dedication of the altar to *Clementia*, and in that year I shall presently insert the most outstanding of all Tiberius' exhibitions of clemency. And it will be recalled that our sources for the years 29 and 30 are meagre in the extreme. But even aside from that consideration, a quite adequate continuity has been demonstrated of Tiberius' possession and exercise of the virtue of clemency.

So we come to our final question—why was an altar erected to *Clementia* in A. D. 28? We have mentioned that our sources record no criminal trial in that year after the conclusion on 1 January of the case of Titius Sabinus with his execution on that day. But our sources are in error; there was another case which fell in that year, a sensational case of high treason which issued in conviction and prompted Tiberius to clemency. The case is involved and important; I have told its story before;[58] but it seems neither too familiar nor too dull to bear retelling.

In the last sixteen years of Augustus' reign plots against his throne gathered successively around his

---

[58] *T. A. P. A.*, 62 (1931), 141-168, and references there; *Criminal Trials,* 75 f., 98-103.

daughter, granddaughter and grandson. When the elder Julia was banished in 2 B. C. for immorality, at least one of her paramours, Iullus Antonius, was punished capitally as guilty of conspiracy, and the elder Pliny says Julia was herself also accused of conspiracy. Six years later Julia's place of exile was changed to Regium instead of the island of Pandateria; a plot had been discovered to rescue her from the island and take her to the armies in Germany. In A. D. 5 Agrippa Postumus was banished " ob ingenium sordidum ac ferox " and the second year after that Augustus obtained a decree of the Senate ordering the perpetual exile of Agrippa under military guard in the island of Planasia. Conspiracy is the probable reason in spite of Tacitus' denial that Agrippa had been guilty of any real offense. About the same time the younger Julia and her husband Lucius Paullus were convicted: she was banished and he executed. And *damnatio memoriae*, which followed the conviction in his case, is clear proof that the charge had been high treason. Twice the attempt was made to abduct Agrippa from his island exile and put him at the head of the German armies—once in the last years of Augustus, again immediately after Augustus' death. Both attempts failed, the latter anticipated by Agrippa's execution. And the elder Julia died in 14 when, says Tacitus, the execution of Agrippa had removed the last hope of success she had.

Others did not at once despair: in Julia's son-in-law, Germanicus, might be found a new leader for the movement. Some of the mutinous troops in Germany offered to follow him to Rome and set him on the throne, but he refused to be disloyal.[59] His wife, Agrippina, had other ideas. She was " hot-headed, rebellious, contumacious and haughty; she nursed her wrath and never concealed her resentments; intolerant of equality, greedy for power, she had put off woman's frailties for man's concerns "; and " she had an ambition as lofty as her lineage." [60] The troops returning from the German campaign of A. D. 15 were preceded by rumor that they had been surrounded and the Germans were about to invade Gaul. Agrippina prevented the cutting of the Rhine bridge in the consequent panic; and she stood at the bridge-head to welcome the returning soldiers with applause and gratitude.[61] Roman opinion was vigorously opposed to women's participation in any activities of the military, and it seems always to have roused suspicion of treasonable intent.[62] " Non enim simplices eas curas, nec adversus externos studia militum quaeri " considered Tiberius. Agrippina had gone among the rank and file, approached the military standards, given largess, dressed her son in soldier's uniform and encouraged the troops to call him affectionally " Little Boot." [63]

For many years after that incident we do not hear of any disloyal activity by Agrippina. Germanicus was withdrawn from Germany and sent to the East whither she accompanied him. The legions of Syria had been wooed by Piso and Plancina, and there is no mention of

[59] Tac., 1. 35. 3 f.; cf. Dio, 57. 4. 2; Suet., 25. 2.

[60] Tac., 1. 33. 5; 4. 12. 5, 7; 4. 53. 1; 4. 54. 2; 6. 25. 3; Dio, 57. 6. 3.

[61] Tac., 1. 69. 1-3.

[62] Id., 2. 55. 5; 3. 33. 3; 12. 37. 6; 12. 56. 5; 12. 57. 5; Hist., 1. 48; Dio, 59. 18. 4.

[63] Tac., 1. 69. 4 f.

any effort by Agrippina at their solicitation. Then
Germanicus died and her sons were too young for plotting in their interests to have point as yet. But on her
return to Rome, at Germanicus' funeral, popular enthusiasm for her was manifested, significantly, in hailing
her as an ornament to her country, *the last survivor of
Augustus' blood*, the embodiment of the good old days.[64]

But after Sejanus' assassination of Drusus in A. D.
23 Tiberius presented Germanicus' two elder sons,
Nero and Drusus, to the Senate as his heirs. A section
of the populace was jubilant at the return to prominence
of Germanicus' family. Agrippina ill concealed her
reviving hopes, and her thirst for power was subject of
gossip and some censure.[65] On 3 January of the next
year the pontiffs included the names of Nero and
Drusus in the *vota pro incolumitate principis*, and the
other priests followed their example. Tiberius summoned the pontiffs; had they acted in response to a
request or threat from Agrippina? No, they had thought
it all up themselves. So Tiberius said " Not guilty, but
don't do it again! " and in the Senate prohibited for the
future such premature honors to the young princes.
Sejanus then asserted that the State was divided as if in
civil war; there was a party of Agrippina, gaining
numbers; the only remedy for the increasing dissension
was the destruction of some of the leaders of Agrippina's
party.[66] Indictment for treason was brought immediately against Gaius Silius and his wife Sosia, and three
years later against Titius Sabinus, a Roman knight.
Silius had commanded the army of Upper Germany
from A. D. 14 to 21, had won *ornamenta triumphalia* in

[64] *Id.*, 3. 4. 3.   [65] *Id.*, 4. 8. 5-8; 4. 12. 1 f., 5.   [66] *Id.*, 4. 17.

15 and suppressed the Gallic rebellion in 21; he was a devoted friend of Germanicus, as was Sosia of Agrippina. Silius committed suicide; both were convicted, with *damnatio memoriae* in the case of Silius; Sosia was exiled.[67]

In 25 Sejanus asked permission to marry Livilla; he wanted, he said, protection for his family against the hostility of Agrippina. Tiberius put him off, but remarked such a marriage would more probably aggravate Agrippina's enmity and divide the imperial household itself into factions.[68]

The next year brought the trial of Claudia Pulchra accused of having conspired against Tiberius. Claudia was the second cousin of Agrippina, who interceded for her kinswoman with characteristic impetuosity and bluntness. She found Tiberius sacrificing to Divus Augustus. It was not consistent, said she, to worship Augustus and persecute his posterity. Not into mute statues had his divine spirit passed; she was his true image, blood of his divine blood; she was aware of her peril and put on mourning. The attack upon Claudia was only a pretext; the real attack was upon herself; Claudia's only offense was too great devotion to her; Claudia had forgotten that Sosia suffered punishment for the same devotion. Tiberius said only: " Do you think you are wronged, because you do not rule? " recognizing the clear implication of her reference to her direct descent from Augustus.[69]

Shortly after, Agrippina fell ill and, when Tiberius called upon her, she asked his permission to remarry. He gave her no answer, discerning that the motive was

---

[67] *Id.*, 4. 18-20. 3.   [68] *Id.*, 4. 39 f.   [69] *Id.*, 4. 52 f.

political. I have conjectured that Asinius Gallus was the prospective husband. Then she suspected Tiberius was going to poison her; Sejanus warned her of it, so we are told. When she was guest at dinner in the palace she refused all food. Tiberius said to Livia it could cause no surprise if he dealt rigorously with one who accused him of trying to poison her.[70]

When Tiberius now retired to Capreae Sejanus warned him of Nero. Nero's freedmen and clients, in haste to acquire power, urged him to assume a bold and confident manner; that was what populace and army wanted, and Sejanus would dare make no counter move. To all this Nero listened without forming any wicked plans, says Tacitus, but he did let fall arrogant and ill-considered words. His every word and act was reported to Sejanus by the prefect's agents or by Nero's wife Julia, through her mother Livilla who was or had been Sejanus' mistress.[71]

In A.D. 27 Agrippina and Nero were placed under military surveillance and Sejanus was daily informed of all details of their lives. According to Tacitus, agents of the prefect advised them to flee to the armies in Germany or seek asylum at the statue of Augustus and beg aid of the Senate and the populace; and then these plans which they would not adopt were charged against them.[72] One wearies and grows suspicious of the recurrent theme of Sejanus' villainy; the plans of the Julian party for twenty years or more, off and on, had included hopes for the support of the German armies; and it is evident there was a group in the Senate and there was a section

[70] *Id.*, 4. 54.   [71] *Id.*, 4. 59. 4-60. 4.   [72] *Id.*, 4. 67. 6.

of the population, which favored Agrippina and her
sons. The schemes are entirely plausible and credible.
And Sejanus' own treason provided the younger Agrippina or any other apologist for the Julian faction with
a ready-made scape-goat and villain.

The same year brought the already mentioned trial
of Titius Sabinus, the equestrian adherent of Germanicus and his family. Tacitus preserves the connection of
this case with Agrippina when he records that Sejanus
named Titius along with Silius and Sosia as a leader of
Agrippina's party who must be destroyed; and this is
confirmed by the elder Pliny, who, though guilty of
inaccurate chronology, says that the trial of Titius was
" ex causa Neronis." Titius was executed for treason on
1 January 28 and Tiberius wrote to the Senate express-
ing his thanks that it had removed a man who was a
danger to the State, and adding that he lived in constant
apprehension because of the suspected plots of his
enemies, whom he did not name. But the Senate dis-
cerned that Agrippina and Nero were meant.[73] Tacitus
evidently considers the obvious persecution of Germanicus' family to be the reason for the Senate's insight;
one may think alternatively of the trials of Silius and
Sosia, Claudia Pulchra and Titius Sabinus, of the public
indiscretions of Agrippina and Nero themselves, and of
the probability that some members of the Senate were
privy to their plans.

Then in 29 Livia died, and according to Tacitus almost at once came Tiberius' letter of indictment against
Agrippina and Nero, for the death of Livia had removed

[73] *Id.*, 4. 68-70; 4. 18. 1; Pliny, *N. H.*, 8. 145.

the last check upon Sejanus and Tiberius. The indictment did not charge conspiracy; overbearing conduct and insolent temper was charged against Agrippina, Nero was accused of unnatural vice and insulting language. The Senate was dumbfounded; certain loyalists called for trial; other senators and especially the magistrates held back, for Tiberius had not made his wishes clear and might later regret any action taken against his daughter-in-law and grandson. So the Senate hesitated. Meantime the populace agitated. They said the indictment was a forgery, and paraded with images of Agrippina and Nero; and pamphlet attacks on Sejanus appeared. Sejanus informed Tiberius that the Senate had not acted on the indictment, that there was disloyal speech and seditious pampleteering and added " what remains, but for them to take the sword and choose as leaders and commanders those whose images they follow as standards? " Tiberius demanded that the case be referred to his own court without prejudice.

Avillius Flaccus, subsequently rewarded with the prefecture of Egypt, prosecuted. Both Agrippina and Nero were convicted and sentenced to exile. In bonds and under heavy military guard, they were removed, Agrippina to Pandateria, Nero to Pontia. Nero was declared an *hostis* by the Senate. Fear of an actual outbreak of armed rebellion, an apprehension justified by the Senate's reluctance to act on the indictment and by the popular demonstration, explains the terms of the indictment and the failure to name the specific charge of conspiracy.[74] There followed other trials which can with

[74] *Criminal Trials,* 98-103, and references there.

more or less certainty or probability be regarded as
connected with those of Agrippina and Nero, notably of
Asinius Gallus and Nero's brother Drusus.[75] Nero died
in his island exile in 31; Asinius Gallus and Drusus in
prison in 33.[76]

Then on 18 October 33 Agrippina committed suicide.
Tiberius reported the fact to the Senate by letter. He
noted the striking coincidence that her death had occurred on the anniversary of Sejanus' execution two years
before. He boasted his clemency that she had not been
executed by strangulation and her body exposed on the
scalae Gemoniae. He asked the Senate to make her
birthday *nefastus*; whether that request was complied
with, we do not know. But the Senate did vote its
thanks for the Emperor's clemency and decree that 18
October, date of the deaths of Sejanus and Agrippina,
should be annually commemorated by a dedication to
Jupiter.[77]

We have said that Tacitus, who alone gives any indication of the date of Agrippina's and Nero's indictment,
places it after Livia's death in A. D. 29. But here the
historian errs. As Charlesworth [78] pointed out many
years ago, there is an explicit and unexceptionable statement of Suetonius that Caligula accompanied Germanicus in Syria, returned from there to live with his
mother until her banishment and then lived in the home
of his great-grandmother Livia over whom, when she
died, he pronounced the funeral eulogy.[79] And if con-

---

[75] *Op. cit.*, 104-107.
[76] Dio, 58. 8. 4; Suet., 54. 2; Tac., 6. 23. 1, 4.
[77] *Id.*, 6. 25.
[78] M. P. Charlesworth, *C. P.*, 17 (1922), 260 f.
[79] Suet., *Cal.*, 10. 1.

firmation were needed, Velleius seems to give it.[80] It
thus becomes evident that the banishment of Agrippina
preceded the death of Livia, which Cortellini has dated
late in A. D. 29;[81] that is *terminus ante quem* for the
trial and conviction of Agrippina and Nero. Pliny's
phrase concerning the case of Titius Sabinus, " ex causa
Neronis,"[82] could be taken as indication that the trial
of Nero preceded even the trial of Titius, occurred as
early as 27. But it seems better to consider Pliny's
chronology at fault than to suppose that Tacitus, by
intention or inadvertence, has moved an important case
two whole years or more from its correct chronological
setting. But I believe we can assign the cases of Agrippina and Nero to their proper year.

Narrating the events of A. D. 28 Tacitus records a
rebellion of the German tribe of Frisii and the defeats
which they inflicted on the Roman forces.[83] Then he
writes: " Hence famous among the Germans was the
Frisian name, while Tiberius concealed our losses, not to
entrust conduct of the war to anyone. Nor was the
Senate concerned whether the borders of the Empire
were dishonored; a domestic panic had preoccupied
their minds [*pavor internus occupaverat animos*], whose
remedy was sought in adulation. So although their
opinion was asked on very different matters, they voted
an altar to Clemency and an altar to Friendship with
flanking statues of Caesar and Sejanus, and with repeated entreaties begged them to show themselves to
public sight."[84]

[80] Vell., 2. 130. 4 f.
[81] *Riv. Stor. Ant.*, 3 (1898), 19.
[82] Pliny, *N. H.*, 8. 145.

[83] Tac., 4. 72 f.
[84] *Id.*, 4. 74. 1-3.

Actual proof is not possible. But it seems to me obvious and indubitable that the " pavor internus " came from the conspiracy of Agrippina and Tiberius' indictment of Agrippina and Nero. Convicted of conspiracy, Agrippina and Nero were not executed, but banished. Five years later when Agrippina died, Tiberius boasted of his clemency in not having executed her and the Senate passed a vote of thanks for that clemency. So too on the original occasion the Senate had recognized that preeminent exhibition of Tiberius' *clementia* and commemorated it by the erection of an altar to *Clementia*.

Successive and numerous manifestations by Tiberius of the imperial virtue of clemency prompted the dedication to him of a shield of clemency and the issue of a commemorative series of coins, probably in the early years of the third decade after Christ; an outstanding instance in A. D. 28 led the Senate to dedicate an altar to the virtue; and there is continual evidence for its possession and exercise by Tiberius up to the case of Herod accused by Agrippa in the last year of Tiberius' reign.

III. *MODERATIO*

Sutherland, writing of the appearance of *Clementia* upon the coinage of Tiberius, says it " is accompanied by the kindred virtue, Moderatio," and describes the latter as " a quality which is frequently combined with Clementia,"[1] instancing, however, only one passage from Suetonius' *Julius*.[2] But he does not make any differentiation between the two kindred virtues; on the contrary, he appears to regard them as very close kin indeed, seeing in Tiberius' conduct of the criminal trials " examples of Moderation and Clemency," and concluding his discussion of those trials which he treats: " In all this Tiberius had shown Moderatio not unmixed with Clementia."[3] I believe, however, study will show that *Moderatio*, while sometimes verging on clemency, is for the most part a separate and distinct virtue, which is strikingly characteristic of Tiberius as Emperor and as man.

Let us commence with a few passages from our ancient sources which show the nature of *moderatio* as an imperial virtue and the recognition of it in Tiberius.

Immediately following Tiberius' acceptance of the imperial position, there was an outburst of senatorial flattery toward Livia; there were motions to style her " parens patriae " or " mater patriae," to add after Tiberius' name the phrase " Iuliae filius." The new Emperor, according to Tacitus, " saying that honors to women should be limited [*moderandos feminarum hono-*

---

[1] Sutherland, *loc. cit.*, 129, 139.
[2] Suet., *Jul.*, 75. 1.   [3] Sutherland, *loc. cit.*, 139.

res] and that he would himself observe the same restraint [*temperantia*] in honors which were conferred upon him, but really fretted with jealousy and taking the exaltation of a woman as a depreciation of himself, did not allow even that a lictor be decreed to her, and prohibited an altar of adoption and other honors of the same sort." [4]

In A.D. 16 Asinius Gallus proposed that elections be held to name the magistrates for the next five years and that legionary commanders, who then held that post before the praetorship, should become praetors designate at once, the Emperor to nominate twelve candidates for each year. Tacitus continues: " There was no doubt that this motion had a deep significance, in fact, touched upon the secrets of empire. But Tiberius spoke as if his power would thereby be increased: it would be *grave moderationi suae* to appoint so many, to defer so many. Hardly was offense avoided with the year-by-year arrangement, although hope for the near future consoled a rejection; how much odium would be felt by those who were put off five years? and how could one foresee what would be a candidate's disposition, family and status after such an interval? Men put on airs enough in one year as magistrates designate; what if they could exercise that prestige for five years? The proposal would multiply the magistrates five times, would subvert the laws which set their own terms on the exercise of candidates' activity and the seeking or holding of magistracies. By this speech, popular in aspect, he retained the substance of power." [5]

Suetonius, quoting a sentence from a speech of Ti-

---

[4] Tac., 1. 14. 1-3; cf. Dio, 57. 12. 4 f.; Suet., 50. 3.
[5] Tac., 2. 36.

berius in the Senate, says that the address was "per-
civilis"; and elsewhere refers to the commencement of
Tiberius' reign, "when he was still seeking to win
men's favor by a pretense of moderation [*moderationis
simulatione*]." [6] The accusation of pretense is familiar
to every student of the reign of Tiberius.

We may note, as preparation for further study of
Tiberius' *moderatio*, some of the distinctive vocabulary
of the virtue. Most frequent are *modus* and its various
derivatives—*modestus* and *modestia, modicus, moderari*
and *moderatio*; but also common are *temperare, temperantia* and *temperamentum, civilis* and, in Greek,
δημοτικός and ἰδιώτης and their derivatives.

Of first interest and importance is the restraint imposed by Tiberius on the honors conferred upon himself.
We have noticed his promise of that moderation just
after his accession; he had already given proof before the promise and on many subsequent occasions
fulfilled it.

When the Senate debated the succession to Augustus,
Tiberius spoke at length "de magnitudine imperii, sua
modestia," and, stating that only Augustus had been
able alone to cope with the administration of the Empire, expressed his willingness to undertake whatever
part of the task the Senate should assign to him. Then
Asinius Gallus asked which part he wished to have
entrusted to him; Tiberius replied that it was "nequa-
quam decorum *pudori* suo" to choose or to avoid any
specific part of that from which he preferred to be
entirely excused.[7] And Velleius describes the "sort of

---

[6] Suet., 28; 57. 1.
[7] Tac., 1. 11. 1; 1. 12. 1-3; cf. Suet., 24; 25. 2.

struggle in the State, of the Senate and Roman people pressing Caesar to succeed to his father's position, of Caesar desiring permission rather to play the part of a citizen equal with the rest than of a *princeps* standing above the others. He was prevailed upon in the end by reason rather than by the honor, since he saw that what he did not undertake to protect would perish. In his case alone, it befell that he should refuse the principate longer almost than others had fought to obtain it." [8] The controversial question of the sincerity or insincerity of this reluctance to accept the imperial position is hardly relevant to our present purpose; but I may, in passing, express my own opinion that it was genuine, and a hope that the conclusions of the present study may be thought to have some bearing as evidence pointing toward such a judgment upon the opening scene of Tiberius' principate.

Suetonius says that " at the beginning he showed himself democratic to a degree [*civilem admodum*] and almost as a private citizen. Of many and very high honors he accepted few and those modest [*modicos*]." [9]

In A. D. 15 " the title of *pater patriae*," narrates Tacitus, " repeatedly urged upon him by the people Tiberius refused, nor did he allow the swearing of an oath to his *acta*, although the Senate so voted, saying that all affairs of mortal men were unsure and the more he attained, the more slippery his footing would be. But he did not win trust in his democratic disposition [*civilis animi*] because he had revived the law of treason." [10]

[8] Vell., 2. 124. 2 (Loeb considerably modified).
[9] Suet., 26. 1.
[10] Tac., 1. 72. 1-3.

The oath to his *acta* had been proposed the preceding year by Valerius Messalla at the time of Tiberius' accession; and at that time he endeavored to make his position clear by eliciting from Messalla the declaration that he made the motion of his own initiative, not at any suggestion from Tiberius.[11] Suetonius and Dio confirm and supplement Tacitus' account concerning the oath to the *acta* and the appellation of *pater patriae*. The biographer quotes two brief excerpts from Tiberius' speech of refusal, and adds Tiberius' declination of the *corona civica*; while both writers record his rejection of the *praenomen imperatoris*.[12]

After Tiberius had relieved a shortage of grain in A. D. 19, the appellation of *pater patriae* was urged again, and again refused. People called him *dominus* and spoke of his *sacrae* or *divinae occupationes*. He replied, " I am *dominus* to my slaves, I am *imperator* to the soldiers, but first citizen to the rest," and suggested that his activities were rather *laboriosae* than divine.[13]

Two years later when the Emperor had been absent temporarily in Campania and was about to return to Rome, Cornelius Dolabella moved that he enter the capital in ovation. Tiberius wrote " that he was not so needy of glory that, after having in his youth conquered some of the fiercest tribes and accepted or declined so many triumphs, he must now in his old age ask an empty honor for a pleasure trip in the suburbs." [14]

---

[11] *Id.*, 1. 8. 5.
[12] Suet., 67. 2-4; 26. 2; Dio, 57. 2. 1; 57. 8. 1, 4; cf. 58. 17. 3.
[13] Tac., 2. 87; Dio, 57. 8. 2; Suet., 27.
[14] Tac., 3. 47. 4 f.

To the year 25 belongs a very significant public declaration of policy by Tiberius. We have in another context used a brief excerpt from Tacitus' summary of it; we shall now quote more largely. Further Spain petitioned to erect a shrine to Tiberius and Livia, following the precedent set in Asia. Tacitus writes: " On this occasion Caesar, firm anyway in disdaining honors and thinking now that he must answer those gossips who accused him of having turned toward vanity, spoke somewhat as follows: ' I know, Senators, that many persons missed my usual steadfastness [*constantia*—and that quality of Tiberius might perhaps repay a little study] because I did not oppose the identical petition recently of the cities of Asia. Therefore, I shall state at once the defense of my former silence and what I have decided for the future. Since the deified Augustus did not forbid the erection in Pergamum of a temple to himself and the city of Rome, I, who observe all that he said or did as binding law, followed the more readily the precedent which he had approved, because with my worship that of the Senate was joined. But although to have allowed it once may be pardoned, to be consecrated in the image of the gods throughout the provinces would be vain and arrogant; and the honor of Augustus will become empty if it is made common by promiscuous flatteries. That I am mortal and perform the functions of men, and that I am satisfied if I fulfill the post of *princeps*, I call you, Senators, to witness and I wish posterity to remember, who will grant enough and to spare of credit to my memory, provided they believe me worthy of my forebears, provident of your interests, firm in danger, and unfearful of enmities incurred for the welfare of the State. . . . These shall be my temples in your hearts, these the most beautiful images, and enduring besides. For those which are built of stone, if the judgment of posterity turns to hatred, are scornfully regarded as tombs. Therefore, I pray that the gods may grant me to the end of my life a tranquil mind understanding the law of men and gods, and that provincials and citizens, when I depart this life, may accord approval and kindly recollection to my deeds and the memory of my name.' And he persisted thereafter even in private conversation in disdaining such veneration of him. Some interpreted this attitude as modesty [*modestia*], many as caused by self-distrust, and some as indication of ignoble soul. For the best of men, they said, desired the highest honors; so Hercules and Liber among the Greeks and Quirinus with us had joined the number of the Gods. Augustus had known better—he had hoped. All else belonged immediately to a *princeps;* one thing must be an unremitting quest—his own fair memory; for in contempt of fame virtues themselves were contemned." [15]

In the same vein had been Tiberius' reply some years before to the people of Gythium when they offered divine honors to him: " I think it fitting that all men in general and your city in particular should reserve honors that befit the gods for the greatness of my father's benefits toward the whole world; for myself, I am satisfied with more moderate honors such as belong to men." [16]

[15] *Id.*, 4. 37 f.
[16] Cf. *infra*, 112, n. 43; the relevant passage is conveniently accessible in L. R. Taylor's " Tiberius' Refusals of Divine Honors," *T. A. P. A.*, 60 (1929), 89, n. 6.

From Dio and Suetonius we learn in particular some of the divine honors which Tiberius thus declined: temples and priests, sacrifices and images; the inherited title of *Augustus*; the celebration of his birthday and its commemoration in the *Fasti*; the renaming of September or his birth-month in his honor—the last rejected with his characteristic wit: "And what will you do if there are thirteen Caesars?"[17]

Nor does it in the least signify, for our present study, that some of these honors were actually bestowed.[18] The announced refusal to accept divine honors represents Tiberius' official policy and is a manifestation of the virtue of *moderatio*; if, despite the official rejection, provincials and even citizens actually bestow the honors, they are, of course, and unavoidably, received, but they are not accepted. This is a distinction with a difference.

After the overthrow of Sejanus, according to Dio, proposals were renewed of the celebration of his birthday and the conferment of the title *pater patriae*, but

[17] Dio, 57. 2. 1; 57. 8. 1, 3; 57. 9. 1 f.; 57. 18. 2; 58. 8. 4; Suet., 26. Cf. Dio, 59. 3. 2.

[18] Miss Taylor, *loc. cit.*, 94 f., discusses Tiberius' subsequent "acceptance" of many honors he had rejected. But Miss Taylor errs in the matter of the inclusion of Tiberius' birthday in the calendar. She writes: "He later had his birthday inscribed in the state calendar (Suet., *Tib.* 5) and it appears in the *Fasti Antiates* which date from the reign of Claudius." Now the words of Suetonius are these: "Sed ut plures certioresque tradunt, natus est Romae in Palatio XVI Kal. Dec. M. Aemilio Lepido iterum L. Munatio Planco conss. per bellum Philippense. Sic enim in fastos actaque in publica relatum est." This passage provides no evidence of the date when "in fastos . . . relatum est." But Dio, in his account of A. D. 40, records a decree of the Senate providing that the birthdays of Tiberius and Drusilla should be observed in the same way as that of Augustus (59. 24. 7). This was doubtless the date also of the entry in the *Fasti* of Tiberius' birthday, and hence its appearance in the *Fasti Antiates*.

Cf. also K. Scott, "Tiberius' Refusal of the title 'Augustus,'" in *C. P.*, 27 (1932), 43-50.

Tiberius again refused to permit any such motion. Likewise, he declined to receive in audience the embassy of senators and knights which came to congratulate him upon the suppression of the conspiracy.[19] And again after the measures in relief of the financial panic of A. D. 33, numerous honors, which Dio does not specify, were voted to him but again refused.[20]

Suetonius adds the remark that, as Emperor, Tiberius held no more than three consulships, one for a few days, one for three months, the other until mid-May.[21] And Velleius writes: "Among the other acts of Tiberius Caesar, wherein his remarkable moderation [*singularis moderatio*] shines forth conspicuously, who does not wonder at this also, that, although he unquestionably earned seven triumphs, he was satisfied with three? " [22] We may discount the example cited, for Augustus, rather than Tiberius, determined the number of his triumphs. But the same historian has an apt summation in the words: " In the case of this man, one does not know which to admire the more, that in courting toils and danger he went beyond all bounds or that in accepting honours he kept within them." [23]

Having set and maintained an example in his own actions, Tiberius imposed the same moderation upon the honors accorded other members of the imperial family, and in other ways restrained the elevation of that family. We have mentioned his refusal to allow Livia to be honored as *mater patriae*. Livia herself had ideas about her own position in the State which Tiberius

[19] Dio, 58. 12. 8; 58. 13. 2.
[20] *Id.*, 58. 22. 1.
[21] Suet., 26. 2.

[22] Vell., 2. 122. 1 (Loeb).
[23] *Id.*, 2. 122. 2 (Loeb).

could not approve. When she wished to banquet senators, knights, and their wives in honor of the dedication of a statue of Augustus, he would not allow it until the Senate gave its approval; then, he entertained the men himself and Livia only the women.[24] "And he repeatedly enjoined her to refrain from activities of importance unbecoming to women, especially after he learned that she had been present at the fire beside the temple of Vesta and had exhorted populace and soldiers to greater efforts." [25] " He was vexed with her because he thought she was trying to hold an equal place with him in public life, and avoided frequent meeting or long, private conversations with her, yet often asked and followed her advice. But when she insisted that a certain citizen be enrolled on the list of jurors, he blocked her by agreeing to do so only on condition of recording officially that he had been coerced by his mother." [26]

The year 16 saw an amusing episode. Lucius Piso summoned the grand lady, Urgulania, to law. She, considering that her friendship with Livia privileged her to stand above the laws, refused to appear but drove to the palace instead. Piso stood his ground in spite of Livia's complaint that it was an indignity and injury to her. Tiberius thought it would be *civile* to indulge his mother thus far—he would go to court and appear in Urgulania's behalf. He set out from the palace, followed at a distance by his bodyguard. People gathered along his route to watch. With perfect composure and exag-

[24] Dio, 57. 12. 5.
[25] Suet., 50. 3.
[26] *Op. cit.*, 50. 2; 51. 1 paraphrased and condensed.

gerated leisure, he carried on various conversations all the way. Meantime, Piso obstinately refused to drop the case as his relatives urged; so Livia ordered his claim to be paid. That was the end of the matter; Piso had won his point and Tiberius had enhanced his reputation.[27]

When his mother died in A. D. 29, the Senate lavished honors on her memory, but Tiberius diminished them " quasi per modestiam," says Tacitus. Dio says the women were ordered to mourn her for a year, with which Tiberius seems not to have interfered, but the arch which the Senate voted, and Tiberius promised to erect, he did not build. Her deification he forbade, asserting she had not wished it.[28]

One of the honors invented for Germanicus after his death was a shield of gold and extraordinary size among those of other authors on the walls of the Palatine. Tiberius said no, the usual size and usual material, for literary excellence had nothing to do with the author's rank.[29] And when he charged the court at the trial of Piso, he concluded, " In this alone have we set Germanicus above the laws, that the inquiry on his death should be in the Curia instead of the forum, before the Senate instead of the praetor's jurors; let all else be conducted with equal restraint [pari modestia]." [30]

His own son Drusus seems to have required a firm hand, for he was disposed to arrogance, license and cruelty. Dio reports that Tiberius once said to him publicly, " While I live, you shall not act with violence or arrogance, and if you try it, not after I'm dead

[27] Tac., 2. 34. 3-7.
[28] Id., 5. 2. 1; Dio, 58. 2. 1-3, 6; Suet., 51. 2.
[29] Tac., 2. 83. 4.
[30] Id., 3. 12. 10.

either." [31] In A. D. 20 at the trial of Aemilia Lepida, Drusus, as consul designate, would normally have expressed his opinion on the sentence first; Tiberius exempted him from that obligation or privilege. Some regarded that action as *civile*, because it relieved the other senators of any necessity to agree with the prince.[32] Two years later, when Drusus received the tribunician authority, there were motions for statues of Tiberius and Drusus, altars to the gods, temples, arches and the like, the designation of that year by the names of the holders of tribunician power instead of the consuls', and the recording of the decrees upon the wall of the Curia in golden letters. But Tiberius modified [*temperavit*] these proposals, specifically criticizing the golden letters as unprecedented and in violation of Roman tradition.[33] Even the "temperavit" of Tacitus is probably an understatement for it appears likely that all the motions were simply vetoed.

We have alluded in another context to Tiberius' disapproval of the inclusion in the *vota* of the names of Nero and Drusus; "the susceptible minds of the young men," he said, "must not be stimulated to arrogance by premature honors." [34] And he seems later to have adjured the Senate similarly with respect to their younger brother, Gaius, the future Emperor.[35]

Tiberius seems, interestingly enough, to have made a special point of funerals in the imperial family, that they should not be elaborate; for in connection with every such funeral, we encounter some manifestation of

[31] Dio, 57. 13. 2.
[32] Tac., 3. 22. 6.
[33] *Id.*, 3. 59. 2; cf. 3. 57. 2 f.

[34] *Id.*, 4. 17. 3; Suet., 54. 1. Cf. *supra*, 52.
[35] Dio, 58. 23. 1.

moderatio. At the death of his brother, the elder Drusus, " he set a limit [*modum*] on the mourning both for himself and everyone else," says Seneca, " and forcing the army into accord with Roman habits of grief, ruled that there must be discipline in mourning as well as in campaigning." [36] Even in the case of Augustus himself, surprisingly, when the senators wished to bear the late Emperor's body on their shoulders, Tiberius excused them from that duty " adroganti moderatione." [37] And the next year, having lost his grandson, the son of Drusus, he would not interrupt his duties, for a ruler must not neglect cares of State on account of personal misfortunes.[38] The imperial family is not imperial at all, but a private family. The funeral of Germanicus was in striking contrast to that which Augustus had given his father, the elder Drusus; people missed even the honors which were usual and due to any person of noble birth.[39] Taking cognizance of the gossip Tiberius issued an edict: " many famous Romans had died for the State; none had been celebrated with such passionate mourning, a great honor to himself and all the rest, if only some measure [*modus*] were observed; for the same conduct was not becoming to the imperial family and to an imperial people as to humble households or small states." [40] After the death of Drusus, he refused again to suspend his usual activities, but finding his consolation in his official duties, attended to the lawsuits of citizens and the petitions of provincials. Entering the Senate, he found that the consuls in sign of

[36] Sen., *ad Polyb.*, 15. 5.
[37] Tac., 1. 8. 6.
[38] Dio, 57. 14. 6.

[39] Tac., 3. 5.
[40] *Id.*, 3. 6. 1 f.

mourning had left their magisterial seats for the benches
of the House, and admonished them of their official
position and their proper place.[41] Again there seems
implicit a denial that the members of the Emperor's
house have official status; they are private persons.
Dio does, it is true, say that Tiberius arranged a state
funeral for Livia, but Tacitus says it was " modicum ";
and once more Tiberius did not abandon the conduct of
public business." [42]

Beyond the restraint upon honors accorded himself
and other members of the imperial family, there was
that upon the extension of government, and upon the
enlarging of the Emperor's powers; corollary of the
latter was consistent effort to make the Senate shoulder
its share of the responsibility of administration, and
scrupulous regard for the position and functions of the
magistrates.

Tiberius tried to forestall the application of the *lex
maiestatis* to libel and slander of himself by a pronouncement in the Senate: " In a free State speech and
thought ought to be free " and " we have not so much
leisure that we ought to involve ourselves in more
affairs; if you open this window, you will allow no other
business to be transacted; for under this pretext the
enmities of all men will be brought before you." [43]

In A. D 20 the Senate debated " de moderanda Papia
Poppaea " and we have seen in another connection that
Tiberius " statuendo remedio " set up a commission of
fifteen senators which resolved many of the law's en-

[41] *Id.*, 4. 8. 2 f.; 4. 13. 1; Dio, 57. 22. 3; Suet., 52. 1.
[42] Dio, 58. 2. 1; Tac., 5. 1. 6; 5. 2. 1.
[43] Suet., 28.

tanglements.[44] Two years later the proposal was put forward to enact sumptuary legislation. The Senate referred the whole question to the Emperor. "But Tiberius," says Tacitus, "after repeatedly pondering whether such unbridled passions could be repressed, whether the repression might do more damage to the State, what an indignity it would be to attempt what could not be accomplished or, if accomplished, would bring disgrace and infamy upon illustrious citizens, finally addressed a communication to the Senate." [45] From Tacitus' summary of this very interesting and important document an excerpt has already been quoted as evidence of Tiberius' *providentia*; it contains also an expression of the opinion to which his ponderings had led him: "If those energetic gentlemen, the aediles, had first consulted me, I rather think I should have urged them rather to let alone full-grown and vigorous vices than to accomplish only the disclosure of what abuses we are not able to cope with." [46] After concluding his account of the whole episode, Tacitus writes: "Tiberius, having obtained a reputation for moderation, because he had checked the rise of accusers, sent a dispatch to the Senate, in which he asked the tribunician authority for Drusus [*fama moderationis parta, quod ingruentis accusatores represserat, mittit litteras ad senatum, quis potestatem tribuniciam Druso petebat*]." [47] Now this sentence Sutherland has regarded as evidence of Tiberius' clemency in the administration of trials for treason. And he comments: " The reference here can scarcely be, as Furneaux was inclined

[44] Tac., 3. 25. 1; 3. 28. 6.   [46] Tac., 3. 53. 2.
[45] *Id.*, 3. 52; cf. Dio, 57. 13. 3 f.   [47] *Id.*, 3. 56. 1.

to think, to Tiberius' preceding letter on the growth
of luxury within the state. That letter was no more
than a piece of sumptuary advice; and only if 'fama
moderationis parta' were not immediately followed
by 'quod ingruentis accusatores represserat,' could
an intelligible connection be maintained." [48] That de-
preciates inordinately the significance of Tiberius' message; but further than that, connection between this
allusion to accusers and the criminal trials is impossibly
remote. The present passage occurs in *Annals* III 56;
chapter 55 is a sketch of the history of luxury from
the battle of Actium to Vespasian; 53 and 54 contain
Tiberius' letter to the Senate, 52 the aediles' complaint which prompted it; chapters 49-51 are the account of the trial of Clutorius Priscus in the preceding
year. Furneaux was quite right; if the sumptuary legislation had been passed, it would have produced a wave
of accusations by informers, such as had resulted from
the operations of the Lex Papia Poppaea.[49] Tiberius,
by forestalling the legislation had checked the threatened rise of informers' activity; hence, Tacitus' phrase
"ingruentis accusatores." But there is more in the
sentence than either Furneaux or Sutherland saw; there
is a contrast between the latter part of the sentence and
the former. For the request of the Emperor that his son
and heir be invested with the tribunician authority was
not an exhibition of *moderatio*, but the contrary.
Having obtained a reputation for *moderatio* by one
action, Tiberius felt it safe (Tacitus would say) to
initiate a proposal which was not characterized by
moderatio, to ask a grant of great power to a member

---

[48] Sutherland, *loc. cit.*, 138.   [49] Cf. Tac., 3. 28. 4-6.

of his family. If the clause " quod ingruentis accusatores represserat " seems to give to *moderatio* an idea of clemency, far more does the proposal of tribunician power for Drusus give the word the meaning of moderation.

There is evident an effort on Tiberius' part to prevent the expansion of the power which the *princeps* possessed. At the opening of his reign, Tacitus says of his commendation of candidates for the praetorship, " Tiberius limiting himself [*moderante*] to the commendation of four persons to be elected without rejection or canvassing," leaving eight to the Senate's election.[50] Velleius says, seemingly of the case of Libo, that Tiberius acted " ut senator et iudex, non ut princeps." [51] At the trial of Piso, Tiberius said, in the words of Tacitus, " If my legate has exceeded the bounds of his authority, has been insubordinate toward his superior commander, has rejoiced in that superior's death and my grief, I shall hate him, banish him from my household, and avenge the personal offense without employing the power of the *princeps*." [52] The same *renuntiatio amicitiae* he invoked many years later against Pomponius Labeo.[53] Especially interesting are his remarks upon the proposal of Cornelius Dolabella in A. D. 22 that no one of scandalous life and known infamy should draw lot for a province, the Emperor to decide who should thus be barred. He said: " Decision should not be based on report. Many had made records in the provinces, the opposite of what had been hoped or feared of them; responsibility spurred some to better

[50] *Id.*, 1. 15. 2; cf. 1. 14. 6.   [52] Tac., 3. 12. 4.
[51] Vell., 2. 129. 2.   [53] *Id.*, 6. 29. 3.

things, others were corrupted. *The Emperor could not of his own knowledge comprehend everything,* nor was it expedient that he be swayed by others' intrigue. The laws regarded past actions because future actions were unpredictable. So the past had ordained that, if delicts went before, penalties should follow after. Let them not alter what had been wisely devised and always approved; *the Emperor had enough of duties, enough, too, of power. Rights were impaired whenever power increased, nor should imperial authority be employed, when procedure was possible under the laws."* [54] And Tacitus, again perversely, comments, " As this democratic attitude [*popularitas*] was rare in Tiberius, it was welcomed with the greater pleasure. And he, practiced in moderation [*prudens moderandi*] if he was not motivated by personal anger," mitigated the sentence of Gaius Silanus, whose trial had prompted Dolabella's motion.[55] Here the following context seems again to suggest the idea of clemency in *moderatio*; but again the significance of " moderandi " is rather to be determined with reference to the preceding context and interpreted as moderation of the Emperor's power and position. Tacitus' description under A. D. 23 of Tiberius' government specifically mentions that the Emperor's land-holdings in Italy were few, his slaves a modest establishment and the number of his freedmen small; and if they had differences with private citizens there was the forum and the law-court. And Dio confirms the last point.[56]

[54] *Id.*, 3. 69. 3-6.
[55] *Id.*, 3. 69. 7 f.
[56] *Id.*, 4. 6. 7; Dio, 57. 23. 5.

With this restraint upon the imperial power went a corresponding endeavor to make Senate and magistrates bear a share of responsibility. In the incident of Agrippa Postumus' execution, Sallustius Crispus warned Livia " ne Tiberius vim principatus resolveret cuncta ad senatum vocando." And Tacitus describes the conduct of affairs at that time in the words, " Tiberius initiated everything through the consuls, as if the old republic were still in being and he undecided to rule." [57] The suggestion is implicit that that manner did not last long; so let us trace it in Tacitus himself and the other sources through the next two decades! Dio elaborates upon the simple statement of Tacitus about the opening of the reign: he records that Tiberius did little or nothing on his own responsibility, referring to the Senate and sharing with it everything, even matters of least importance; that in the Senate he gave his own opinion and allowed others to speak theirs; that he was sometimes in the minority when the vote was taken. And elsewhere he makes the general statement that Tiberius was especially insistent that the Senate should meet as often as it was supposed to, that members be prompt in attendance and not leave the sessions early.[58] When Drusus faced the mutinous legions in Pannonia, he told the troops their major demands must be referred to the Senate.[59] Both Tacitus and Dio inform us that when he attended the praetor's court, he did not allow that magistrate to give up his curule chair but himself sat to the side of the platform.[60] When the unruly conduct

[57] Tac., 1. 6. 6; 1. 7. 4.
[58] Dio, 57. 7. 2-5; 58. 21. 2; cf. Suet., 31. 1.
[59] Tac., 1. 25. 3; 1. 26. 2.
[60] Id., 1. 75. 1; Dio, 57. 7. 6; Suet., 33.

of actors was debated in the Senate in A. D. 15, there
were motions to give the praetors the right to flog them;
a tribune interceded and was attacked in a speech by
Asinius Gallus; Tiberius said nothing because, according
to Tacitus, " he allowed these semblances of liberty to
the Senate." [61] Six years later, Tiberius informed the
Senate that the renewal of Tacfarinas' rebellion in
Africa made it necessary that the proconsul of that
province be a man with military capacity. The Senate
decreed that the *princeps* might select the man to whom
the province and the war should be entrusted. Tiberius
then nominated two between whom the Senate might
choose, but censured the senators for throwing all their
responsibilities upon the *princeps*.[62]   The next year
while, as Tacitus says, " consolidating the power of the
principate by the grant to Drusus of tribunician power,
he allowed the Senate the appearances of the good old
days by sending them the petitions of the provinces."
So the senators listened to embassies from the Greek
cities claiming for their various temples the right of
asylum. And it is interesting to note that the senators
wearied of listening, referred the rest of the business to
the consuls with instructions to report back their recom-
mendations to the House.[63] Tacitus, in his summary of
the first ten years again, records that public business
and important private affairs were administered by the
Senate; that there was free speech in the House and
when adulation appeared, Tiberius repressed it; that
candidates for magistracies were selected with regard for
their birth, their military and civil distinction, and
better candidates could not have been found; that

[61] Tac., 1. 77. 1-3.   [62] *Id.*, 3. 32. 1, 3; 3. 35. 1.   [63] *Id.*, 3. 60. 1; 3. 63. 2.

consulship and praetorship bore their proper aspect and even minor magistracies exercised their due authority; the laws except that of *maiestas* (and the exception is not justified) had salutary enforcement.[64] All this is confirmed by Suetonius who says he produced a sort of appearance of liberty by preserving to the Senate and the magistrates their pristine majesty and authority; nothing was too important nor too unimportant to be referred to the Senate—revenues, monopolies, building, rebuilding, levy and discharge of troops, disposition of legions and auxiliaries, prolongation of commands and extraordinary appointments, diplomatic correspondence with foreign potentates; everything was done through the magistrates and by normal procedure; an embassy from Africa, when the Emperor was slow to handle their business, went to the consuls to complain, such was the importance of the chief magistrates; and army commanders received rebuke for not reporting their campaigns to the Senate.[65] When in A. D. 23 he made Nero and Drusus the wards of the Senate after the death of their uncle Drusus, and then, in Tacitus' words, "recurred to the silly and often derided talk of restoring the republic, and his wish that the consuls or someone else would take over the government," he deserved on his record more credence and sympathy than he received. The historian says he destroyed by this statement trust in what he had said sincerely and honestly.[66] But Tiberius had said when he accepted the principate that it was a slavery, but he would bear it " until I come to the

[64] *Id.*, 4. 6. 2 f.; 4. 15. 3. On the law of *maiestas* and its administration cf. *Criminal Trials, passim*, and especially 190-196.

[65] Suet., 30; 31. 2; 32. 1.

[66] Tac., 4. 9. 1.

time when you may think it fair to give an old man some rest.[67] Dio mentions that after the overthrow of Sejanus, Tiberius ordered all accusations lodged with the Senate, and two years later all documents in his possession or that of his prefect Macro having to do with trials were delivered to the Senate.[68] In 32 his censure of Senate and magistrates for their indifference while the populace rioted over the shortage of grain elicited a decree and consular edicts couched in terms of old-fashioned austerity. But his own silence, which he had thought was *civile*, was interpreted as arrogance.[69]

Tiberius' care that taxes in the provinces should not be oppressive, I have chosen to include at this point, regarding it as *moderatio*. For Suetonius commences a section with the statement: " He exhibited a like moderation also in the case of less important persons and affairs "; and concludes his list of examples with this instance: " When provincial governors urged burdensome taxes for the provinces, he answered by rescript that it was the part of the good shepherd to shear his flock, not to flay it." [70] Suetonius here apparently generalizes, *more suo*, from the case of Aemilius Rectus, the prefect of Egypt, which Dio records in almost identical terms.[71] It is interesting to note in passing, that Suetonius classifies taxation among the minor business of administration! That this was no solitary occurrence,

---

[67] Suet., 24. 2.

[68] Dio, 58. 16. 3; 58. 21. 3.

[69] Tac., 6. 13. 2-4. The Senate's share in the responsibility for the administration of the army, I have discussed rather more fully and from a different point of view in " Tiberius' Reversal of an Augustan Policy," *T. A. P. A.*, 71 (1940), 532-536.

[70] Suet., 32. 2.

[71] Dio, 57. 10. 5.

however, several passages in Tacitus make clear. In
A. D. 15 Achaea and Macedonia petitioned a reduction of
their tax burden and they were accordingly transferred
from senatorial to imperial administration. Two years
later Syria and Judaea made the same appeal, though
we are not informed whether or what action was taken
in their case. But it is stated that when the legate
Quintus Veranius instituted provincial government in
Cappadocia, the taxes imposed by Rome were made
lower than those the country had paid to its former
kings. And Tacitus, writing of A. D. 23, says up to that
year Tiberius " made provision that the provinces
should not be agitated by new taxes and should carry
the old ones free of avarice or cruelty on the part of
the governors." [72] Tacitus' employment of the verb
providere as well as the nature of this concern for the
provincials would, of course, justify the classification
of this moderation of the tax burdens as *providentia*,
the Emperor's fatherly care of his subjects.

Moderatio it was also that Tiberius allowed the name
of the original builder to remain, and without adding
his own, on structures which he repaired or restored.
Dio states this in the broadest terms, asserting it not
only of the restoration of Augustus' works but as an
unchanging principle followed always by Tiberius.
Velleius has the most effusive notice of it, as one would
expect, exclaiming, " *Quam magnifico animi temperamento* he restored the works of Pompey when they were
destroyed by fire." Tacitus, recording the same instance
of his work of restoration, has the brief and sober
" manente tamen nomine Pompei." [73]

[72] Tac., 1. 76. 4; 2. 42. 7; 2. 56. 4; 4. 6. 7.
[73] Dio, 57. 10. 1 f.; Vell., 2. 130. 1; Tac., 3. 72. 4.

It would perhaps be surprising if so prominent a characteristic of Tiberius' public and official conduct were not strikingly noticeable in his personal and private manner and speech as well. Certainly it is abundantly manifest there also. Augustus had had confidence in Tiberius' *modestia* as well as in his own prestige when he appointed him to share the tribunician power.[74] In Rhodes he was content with a modest house and a hardly more elaborate suburban villa, and his mode of life was " civile admodum," unattended as he was by lictor or courier, and associating with the Greeks of the city almost on equal terms. Suetonius adds a pleasant anecdote. " Once in planning the disposition of his day he chanced to say he would like to visit the sick of the city. He was misunderstood by his suite, and they gave orders that all the sick be brought to a public colonnade and there arranged in groups according to their various maladies. Quite taken aback and long uncertain what to do, he finally made the rounds apologizing to each for what had happened, even to the humblest and most insignificant." And during his sojourn in Rhodes, he made but a solitary exercise of his tribunician authority.[75]

Notoriously he set a very modest table, serving warmed-over viands of the preceding day even to guests, censuring his son Drusus for his dislike of cabbage, horrified at the fantastic prices paid by others for mullets and for Corinthian table-ware.[76]

He rose from his seat at the approach of the consuls, made himself accessible and approachable to the sen-

[74] Tac., 3. 56. 4.
[75] Suet., 11. 1-3; cf. 32. 2.
[76] *Id.*, 34. 1; Pliny, *N. H.*, 19. 137.

ators, addressing them with almost excessive politeness, maintained with his own friends the relations usual in private life, lending them his support in the law-courts, sacrificing with them on festal occasions, visiting them when they were sick.[77]

The words of his edict convoking the Senate after Augustus' death were few and " sensu permodesto." [78] At the trial of Libo he read the indictment in so restrained a manner (*ita moderans*) as to appear neither to mitigate nor aggravate the charges; so, too, at the trial of Piso, his address to the senatorial court was " meditato temperamento." [79] Lucius Piso's outburst of indignation at conditions in the courts and his *rencontre* with Urgulania and Livia, Tiberius accepted " civiliter," though Tacitus would have us believe he bore a grudge for eight years and had his revenge on Piso in the end.[80] His commendation of Drusus for the tribunician power was moderate and free of exaggerations.[81] When Brutus' widow, Junia, died, her will was found to contain complimentary reference to practically everybody who was anybody in the State except Tiberius. He took the studied omission " civiliter." [82] Tiberius' reply to Sejanus' request for the hand of Livilla rehearsed " modice " the prefect's services.[83] When a senator proposed, rather impudently to Tiberius' opinion, that a senatorial bodyguard be assigned to the Emperor, the

[77] Dio, 57. 11. 1, 3, 7; Suet., 29.
[78] Tac., 1. 7. 6.   [80] *Id.*, 4. 21. 1 f.
[79] *Id.*, 2. 29. 2; 3. 12. 1.   [81] *Id.*, 3. 56. 6.
[82] *Id.*, 3. 76. 2 f. Radin has recently commented, " the emperor, so ostentatiously passed over, was a special sort of person. To Tiberius Caesar Augustus, this example of aloof and grim pertinacity was rather attractive than otherwise," *Marcus Brutus*, 237.
[83] *Tac.*, 4. 40. 1.

rejection of the motion contained only moderate criticism ("verbis moderans") of its sponsor.[84] In 32 a tribune brought before the Senate the matter of a Sibylline book which one of the quindecimvirs demanded should be included in the official canon; Tiberius rebuked the tribune "modice" as ignorant of tradition because of his youth, while severely censuring the priest who ought to have known better and had not followed the required procedure in the matter.[85]

Final manifestation of Tiberius' *moderatio* is his hatred of flattery. We have already quoted one statement of his suppression of adulation from Tacitus' famous summary of the first ten years.[86] There are several other passages equally specific. Suetonius devotes a chapter to that rubric. Tiberius would not allow a senator to approach his litter either to pay his respects or on business; the biographer narrates the incident of Haterius, which we have recounted in another connection—how Tiberius was so anxious to escape from the suppliant's embrace of his knees that he fell over backwards. And anyone who spoke too flatteringly in conversation or public address was unhesitatingly interrupted, rebuked and corrected on the instant; Suetonius illustrates the point by Tiberius' amendments of the words *dominus, auctor* and *sacrae occupationes*.[87] The Emperor's criticism of those words, which Tacitus also records, evokes from that historian the comment: "Speech was constricted and risky under an Emperor who feared freedom and hated flattery."[88] Elsewhere he has a fuller statement of the same idea: "But that

---

[84] *Id.*, 6.2.6.
[85] *Id.*, 6.12.1 f.
[86] *Supra*, 79.

[87] Suet., 27.
[88] Tac., 2.87.2.

age was so tainted and besmirched with flattery that not only the outstanding men of the State, who must preserve their distinction by obsequiousness, but all the consulars, a large part of the ex-praetors and many even of the humbler senators vied with one another in rising to make shameful and extravagant motions. It is related that Tiberius, whenever he left the House, habitually remarked, ' Men fit to be slaves! ' Evidently even he, who was opposed to the people's freedom, wearied of such abject submissiveness by his slaves." [89] Tacitus' conviction of Tiberius' opposition to liberty must, I believe, be remnant of his preconceptions of that Emperor's character and government, which, Marsh has cogently argued, he was unable to discard completely when the evidence of his own studies failed to bear them out.[90] A final passage has the added interest that it shows the detestation of flattery still active late in the reign, A.D. 35 to be precise. Fulcinius Trio made an attack in his will upon the praetorian prefect Macro, on Tiberius' principal freedmen and on the Emperor himself, charging that his mind was impaired by senility and his continued residence in Capreae was tantamount to exile. When the heirs would have concealed the contents of the testament, Tiberius ordered it read. Tacitus was undecided whether this was " an ostentatious display of tolerance of free speech and a contempt for attacks upon his own good fame, or whether, having long been ignorant of Sejanus' crimes, he now preferred to publicize attacks however worded, and be apprised, even insultingly, of the truth, which adulation prevents one's learning." [91]

[89] Id., 3. 65. 2-4.   [90] The Reign of Tiberius, 284-288.   [91] Tac., 6. 38. 2 f.

This *Moderatio*—the strict limitation of the honors accepted for himself or the members of his family; the effort to prevent the family from assuming, or having thrust upon it, imperial position; the endeavor to moderate the tendency to expand the powers of government in general and more especially of the Emperor in particular; the determination that the Senate and the old magistracies should be held in honor, should accept responsibilities and perform real functions; the care to make taxation tolerable; the restraint in personal manner and speech, and the vehement dislike of adulation— exhibited throughout the duration of his reign, was recognized by his people and commemorated by the dedication of an honorary shield of moderation and an issue of coins which depicted that shield with the Emperor's portrait and bore the legend " Moderationi." [92] The honors were well deserved.

* * * * *

Liberalitas is linked with *Providentia* by their sharing of the public works and the grain supply. The moderation of taxation is common to *Providentia* and *Moderatio*. And *Moderatio* seems sometimes tangential, at least, to *Clementia*. *Liberalitas, Providentia, Clementia* and *Moderatio*—imperial virtues all, all possessed by Tiberius, and all consistently manifest from the commencement of his reign to its termination more than twenty-two years later. Not without good reason was it that Valerius Maximus referred to Tiberius as " optimus princeps," that Aulus Fabius Fortunatus, *Augustalis* of the town of Rignum, in A.D. 32 or 33 made dedication

[92] *B.M.C.*, Tib., 90. Cf. *supra*, 38.

" principi optumo ac iustissimo, conservatori patriae pro salute et incolumitate eius," and that the consular Gaius Fulvius made vows for the well-being " principis optimi et iustissimi." [93] Trajan was not the first *Optimus Princeps.*

Liberalitas, Providentia, Clementia—these virtues appear in legends on the coins of many other Emperors in Roman history. *Moderatio*, though it recurs in literature, as notably in Pliny's panegyric on Trajan, never appears again upon the coins. It is Tiberius' own peculiar and distinctive virtue. It does him great honor—the *Moderatio* of Tiberius.

[93] Val. Max., 2 praef.; Dess. 159 (= *C. I. L.*, XI, 3872); 3783 (= *C. I. L.*, VI, 3675 = 30856).

DRUSUS JULIUS CAESAR

THE AVIGNON HEAD

(*Römische Mitteilungen*)

DRUSUS JULIUS CAESAR

I. YOUTH AND FAMILY

The marriage of Tiberius Claudius Nero and Vipsania Agrippina united an interesting group of families. Tiberius' father was descended through a long line of patrician Claudii from Appius Claudius Caecus; his mother, Livia, like her husband a descendant of the blind censor Claudius, but bearing the name of the Livii Drusi into which family her Claudian father had passed by adoption. Vipsania was the daughter of Agrippa by his marriage with Pomponia, the daughter of Atticus. The marriage was a political one, arranged when the bride was a year old, but an eminently successful and happy one.[1] Sole issue of the union was he whom we call Drusus Julius Caesar, descendant of patrician and noble Claudii, equestrian Pomponii and the more humble Vipsanii.

The day of Drusus' birth is definitely known, 7 October, commemorated in the calendar of Cumae;[2] but the year is doubtful. Clearly he was younger than Germanicus, who was born 24 May, 15 B. C., even though his name does precede that of Germanicus on coins of Sardes.[3] Borghesi[4] deduced from the date of Drusus' quaestorship that he was born in 15. Mommsen,[5] however, citing the case of Caligula, quaestor in his twenty-third year, as evidence that one might reach that office

---

[1] Suet., 3; 7. 2; Nepos, *Att.*, 19; Tac., 1. 12. 6.
[2] Dess., 108 (= *C. I. L.*, X, 3682 = 8375 = I², p. 229, and cf. p. 331).
[3] *B. M. C.*, *Lydia*, Sardes, #104-112.
[4] *Œuvres Complètes*, VIII, 13.
[5] *Hermes*, 17 (1882), 634 (= *Ges. Schr.*, IV, 262).

before he was twenty-five even without a law advancing his eligibility, set Drusus' birth less definitely—between 15 and 12. These *termini* are provided respectively by Germanicus' birth and Vipsania's divorce which occurred in 12 after she had borne Drusus.[6] There are two other pieces of evidence which bear upon the date, if they do not afford more satisfactory conclusions. In A. D. 22 when Tiberius asked the tribunician power for Drusus, he told the Senate that Drusus was then of the age at which he had himself received the same power at Augustus' hands.[7] Tiberius was in his thirty-sixth year when, in 6 B. C., he was first invested with the tribunician authority.[8] If Tiberius' remark be interpreted literally, it leads to the conclusion that his son was born in 15. But on the other hand in A. D. 17, when Tiberius asked the appointment of Germanicus to the East, he gave as the reason for his selection, according to Tacitus, that he was himself too old and Drusus not yet old enough.[9] Placing Drusus' birth in 15 makes him Germanicus' junior by only four and a half months; he would then be old enough for any commission for which Germanicus was old enough, and Tiberius' statement would be meaningless.

It remains, then, impossible to fix with any confidence the year of Drusus' birth as 15, 14 or 13 (I rather incline to choose 13). And what name he was given at birth we do not know; we can call him only by the name which he received when Augustus arrogated Tiberius—Drusus Julius Caesar—though one might guess that he had been called Tiberius Claudius Drusus.

[6] Suet., 7. 2; Dio, 54. 31. 2.
[7] Tac., 3. 56. 7.
[8] Dio, 55. 9. 4.
[9] Tac., 2. 43. 1.

Of Drusus' early years we hear little indeed. In 12
B. C. Tiberius was compelled to divorce his beloved
Vipsania to become engaged to Julia, whose second husband, Agrippa, had died early in that year. Vipsania
became the wife of Asinius Gallus, who is said [10] to have
claimed that Drusus was his son, though it is difficult
to see what plausibility could have been given to such
a claim. When, in the next year, Tiberius married Julia,
the boy Drusus acquired a step-mother of few virtues
and easy virtue, three step-brothers, Gaius and Lucius
his elders, and Agrippa Postumus an infant born the
year before, and a step-sister of about his own age,
Agrippina (she was born in October of 15, 14, or 13),
all four soon or late ill-fated like himself.

His father, certainly, he seldom saw. From 12 to 10
Tiberius spent most of his time with the army in Pannonia; in 9 and 8, he was in Germany. After being in
Rome as consul during 7, he retired to Rhodes the next
year, only returning to the capital in A. D. 2. The next
year but one commenced the long series of campaigns
in Germany and Pannonia, and Tiberius spent only the
winters in Rome until his triumph late in 12. Drusus
was then in his middle twenties and had already, as
we shall see, held the quaestorship.

We hear of Drusus' intimate association with Marcus
Julius Agrippa, who was being reared in the home of
Antonia,[11] Drusus' aunt by marriage. The friendship
with the Jewish prince endured as long as Drusus lived.
We do not hear later that Agrippa borrowed money
from Drusus, but it seems unlikely that the latter could

[10] Dio, 57. 2. 7.
[11] Jos., *Ant.*, 18. 143; M. P. Charlesworth, *Five Men*, 5 f.

have been thus exceptional among the king's friends! Since Josephus states that comradeship between the two youths ante-dated 4 B. C., one wonders whether, when Tiberius retired to Rhodes in 6 B. C., Julia and Drusus went to live with Antonia. If so, the boy would thus have come into association not only with Agrippa, but with his three first cousins, Germanicus who was to become his brother, Claudia Livia Julia (commonly known as Livilla) whom he was later to marry, and Tiberius, the future Emperor Claudius, with which *portentum hominis* [12] Antonia would doubtless have forbidden him to play.

We know no more of the boy until his father's return from Rhodes in A. D. 2 not long before the death of Lucius Caesar, which occurred on 20 August.[13] Drusus now assumed the *toga virilis*, escorted to the forum by Tiberius; he was between fourteen and sixteen years of age.[14] He might now have his first real acquaintance with his father, for Tiberius seems to have remained in Rome, living privately and very quietly,[15] until the middle of A. D. 4. His home also was changed now, whether or not he had been living with Antonia during his father's retirement in Rhodes; for Tiberius moved [16] from the house in the *Carinae*, which had formerly belonged to Pompey,[17] to one in the gardens of Maecenas on the Esquiline.[18]

---

[12] Suet., *Claud.*, 3. 2.
[13] *Prosop.*², C, 941 (p. 222 *med.*); Suet., 14. 1; Vell., 2. 103. 1; Dio, 55. 10a. 10; *Fasti Antiates, C. I. L.*, I², p. 248, cf. p. 326.
[14] Suet., 15. 1.
[15] *Ibid.*
[16] *Ibid.*
[17] Cf. Platner-Ashby, *Topogr. Dict. of Anc. Rome*, 187 f.
[18] *Op. cit.*, 269.

The deaths of Lucius Caesar in A. D. 2 and Gaius in the second year following brought in their train Augustus' arrogation of Tiberius and Agrippa Postumus, and the former's prior arrogation of Germanicus on 26 June, A. D. 4.[19] Drusus thus acquired a grandfather, an uncle and a brother, and was indicated as a possible future heir to the Empire, but one to whom Germanicus was preferred.

About the same time, apparently, Drusus married Livilla, his first cousin, the widow of his step-brother Gaius Caesar. Tacitus says of her: " formae initio aetatis indecorae, mox pulchritudine praecellebat."[20] We may, therefore, suppose that at the time of her second marriage she was a quite beautiful young woman.

Four children were born of the marriage. There was a daughter, Julia, born evidently soon after the marriage, for in A. D. 20 she was married to her first cousin, Nero, the son of Germanicus; following his death in exile, A. D. 31, she was betrothed to Sejanus, but after his overthrow and execution became the wife of Rubellius Blandus in 33, and ten years later fell victim to Messalina.[21] The second child was a son, who, Ovid indicates, was alive and well in A. D. 12/13, and whose death in 15 is recorded by Dio and Velleius.[22] That is all we know of him and modern writers, with a single excep-

---

[19] Vell., 2. 104. 1; 2. 112. 7; Suet., 15. 2; Tac., 1. 3. 3; 12. 25. 2; Gaius, 1. 107; Justinian, *Instit.*, 1. 11. 11; *Fasti Amit.*, C. I. L., I², p. 243, cf. p. 320.

[20] Tac., 4. 3. 3.

[21] *I. G. R. R.*, IV, 325 (at Pergamum); Tac., 3. 29. 4; Dio, 58. 7. 5; Zon., 11. 2; cf. Nipperdey *ad Tac.*, 5. 6; Tac., 6. 27. 1; 13. 32. 5; 13. 43. 3; Dio, 58. 21. 1; 60. 18. 4; Sen., *Apoc.*, 10; Suet., *Claud.*, 29. 1; Incert. Auct., *Oct.*, 944.

[22] Ovid, *Pont.*, 2. 2. 75; Dio, 57. 14. 6; Vell., 2. 130. 3; the last passage Dessau refers to the death of the twin in A. D. 23, *Prosop.* L, 211.

tion, seem completely to have overlooked him.[23] Then in A. D. 19 twin sons were born, to the enormous delight of their grandfather, the Emperor.[24] The date has been subject of some controversy. Hirschfeld [25] argues that Tacitus has inserted the event at this point to contrast pathetically with the death of Germanicus, and that, since the surviving twin was still *praetextatus* at the death of Tiberius eighteen years later, it must have occurred at least a year, perhaps longer, thereafter. Dessau [26] denies the validity of the argument (as did also Furneaux), but having decided upon the date " wohl Anfang 20 n. Chr." without any argument at all, then writes " die 19 oder 20 n. Chr. geborenen Zwillinge." Tacitus [27] writes of A. D. 19: " Ceterum recenti adhuc maestitia (*sc.* for Germanicus' death) . . . Livia . . . duos . . . simul enixa est." Germanicus had died on 10 October, news of it would have reached Rome by late November, if not indeed earlier, and mourning continued until the end of the Saturnalia on 17 December.[28] This seems to me to point to December of 19 for the birth of the twins; not conclusively to be sure, but the arguments for rejecting the year 19 certainly are not acceptable. The boys were called Tiberius (Gemellus) and, apparently, Germanicus.[29]

[23] Neither the *Prosopographia* nor the articles in Pauly-Wissowa on Drusus and Livilla contain mention of him; Baker, Charlesworth, Ciaceri and Marsh all pass him by; Gelzer's article on Tiberius in Pauly-Wissowa has caught Dio's solitary allusion to him.

[24] Tac., 2. 84.

[25] *Hermes*, 25 (1890), 365-373 (= *Kl. Schr.*, 857 ff.).

[26] *Gesch. d. röm. Kaiserz.*, II, i, 27, n. 1, and 33, and cf. Furneaux, *ad Tac.*, 2. 84. 1.

[27] 2. 84. 1.

[28] *Fasti Antiates*, *C. I. L.*, I², p. 249, cf. p. 331; cf. XIV, 4534; Suet., *Calig.*, 6. 2; cf. Tac., 2. 82; Charlesworth, *Trade Routes*, 44 and notes.

[29] *I. G. R. R.*, III, 997; Dess., 170 (= *C. I. L.*, V, 4311).

Tiberius was jubilant and announced the event in the Senate, asserting that never before had twins been born in a Roman family of comparable station.[30] Evidently at this time the Emperor harbored no doubts of the infants' paternity, as it is alleged he later did when at the end of his life he was pondering the problem of the succession.[31] His enthusiasm was doubtless due in great part to his devotion to the cult of the Dioscuri, and the connection of that cult with the institution of the *principes iuventutis* and the imperial succession.[32] The cult of the twins as the Dioscuri appears in Ephesus and at Salamis in Cyprus.[33] Hence, also, certainly the issue of a *sestertius* from the mint of Rome commemorating the twins with a charming type.[34] Germanicus lived only four years or less, dying in the year of his father's assassination, 23; Tiberius, joint heir with his cousin Gaius to the Empire, was put out of the way by him in 37.[35] Livilla was honored in a dedication at Brixia as the mother of the twins; there is extant also a dedication to Tiberius at Alba Pompeia, another of unknown provenience, and his epitaph in Rome.[36]

It has been usual to consider the marriage of Drusus

---

[30] Tac., 2. 84. 2.

[31] Suet., 62. 3; Dio, 57. 22. 4b; 58. 23. 2.

[32] G. P. Baker, *Tiberius Caesar*, 198 and n. 1; and more especially, K. Scott in *C. P.*, 25 (1930), 158-161.

[33] *S. E. G.*, IV, 515; *I. G. R. R.*, III, 997.

[34] *B. M. C.*, Tib., 95-97 and plate 24. 6. Why the type of the twins is not considered the obverse, I do not quite understand. Cf. *C. A. H.*, *Plates* IV, 200, g.

[35] Tac., 4. 15. 1; Suet., *Calig.*, 23. 3; 29. 1; Dio, 59. 8. 1; Philo, *Leg.*, 23-31; *in Flacc.*, 10.

[36] Dess., 170 (= *C. I. L.*, V, 4311); 171 (= *C. I. L.*, V, 7598); *A. E.*, 1933, 94; Dess., 172 (= *C. I. L.*, VI, 892). Another inscription, *C. I. L.*, IX, 2201, seems to honor Vipsania as grandmother of the twin great-grandsons of Augustus.

and Livilla a happy one, although Marsh and Baker have their doubts.[37] The only evidence for their happiness known to me is Drusus' statement in a senatorial debate two years before his death, that he would be reluctant to undertake provincial commands " if he must be separated from his beloved wife, the mother of their many common children," and the verses of the anonymous *Octavia*;

> " Felix thalamis Livia Drusi natisque ferum
> Ruit in facinus poenamque suam." [38]

That leaves me quite unconvinced in view of the facts that against Livilla were alleged adulteries with her physician and confidant, Eudemus, with Sejanus whose accomplice she became in the murder of her husband, and with Mamercus Aemilius Scaurus,[39] and that Drusus' own character, as we shall see, was not one to contribute markedly to his wife's felicity.[40]

Of Drusus' relations with other members of the family we are more or less informed in the cases of his brother and sister-in-law, Germanicus and Agrippina, his nephews, Nero and Drusus, and his father, Tiberius. Tacitus, recording in the year 17 that the court was divided by feelings of favor toward Germanicus or Drusus, states categorically that relations between the two were none the less harmonious in the extreme— " Sed fratres egregie concordes et proximorum certaminibus inconcussi." [41] It used to be customary to cite as corroboration of the historian's assertion coins and inscriptions naming the two princes as φιλάδελφοι θεοί and

---

[37] F. B. Marsh, *The Reign of Tiberius*, 163; Baker, *op. cit.*, 222.
[38] Tac., 3. 34. 13; Incert. Auct., *Oct.*, 942 f.
[39] Pliny, *N. H.*, 29. 20; Tac., 4. 3. 3 f.; 6. 29. 6.
[40] Cf. *infra.*, chap. 4.   [41] Tac., 2. 43. 7.

the like;[42] but it is now recognized that these represent their identification as *principes iuventutis* with the Dioscuri, to which we shall later recur.[43] But without that documentary confirmation Tacitus' statement remains acceptable, and it is borne out by the facts that Drusus and Germanicus united in supporting the latter's relative, Haterius Agrippa, in 17 to succeed Vipstanus Gallus deceased in his praetorship,[44] and that Germanicus visited his brother in Delmatia when he was *en route* to Greece to take up his eastern command later in the same year.[45] When Agrippina returned to Italy with the ashes of her husband early in the year 20, Drusus journeyed as far as Tarracina to meet her;[46] but this may perhaps be discounted as an official mission without motives of personal interest. And finally Cn. Piso found Drusus grieving at Germanicus' death, not rejoicing at the removal of a rival for the succession.[47] But the ambitious Agrippina certainly shed no tears at the death of Drusus which cleared the way for the advancement of her sons.[48] Her two elder sons, Nero and Drusus, after the death of their father, Tiberius had commended to the care of their uncle, and when the young Drusus came of age, Tiberius praised his son for the fatherly benevolence he had shown to his nephews; Tacitus adds his testimony to the truth of Tiberius' remark: "Nam Drusus, quamquam arduum sit eodem loci potentiam et concordiam esse, aequus adulescentibus aut certe non adversus habebatur."[49]

[42] *E. g.*, Gardthausen, in P. W., X, 432, and Kroll, in P. W., X, 451.
[43] Cf. *infra*, 103 f.
[44] Tac., 2. 51; cf. *infra*, 117 f.
[45] Tac., 2. 53. 1.
[46] *Id.*, 3. 2. 4.
[47] *Id.*, 3. 8. 1, 3.
[48] *Id.*, 4. 12. 1 f.
[49] *Id.*, 4. 4. 3; cf. 4. 8. 6.

But with his father, Drusus' relations cannot have been altogether happy, for the *moderatio* of Tiberius was not characteristic of his son. Dio affirms that Tiberius was devoted to him; Tacitus, that the Emperor preferred him over Germanicus as the son of his own blood. But Suetonius asserts that Tiberius did not greatly love his son.[50] Between " he loves him " and " he loves him not " one finds it rather difficult to choose. Certain it is that we hear much of the father's criticism and repression of the son; but that does not, of course, prove a lack of paternal love. Dio reports that Tiberius rebuked him privately and publicly for cruelty and licentiousness and that on one occasion he said to him in public, " So long as I live, you shall not act with violence and arrogance, and if you dare try it, not after I'm dead either." [51] In A. D. 15 Drusus presided over games given in his name and that of Germanicus, and his excessive pleasure in the bloodshed of the spectacle was noticeable; it was said, according to Tacitus, that this provoked his father's censure. This attitude of Tiberius refutes, if refutation is necessary, the malicious gossip, recorded only to be rejected by Tacitus, that Tiberius gave Drusus opportunity to display his cruelty and thus rouse the enmity of the populace.[52] Tacitus likewise contemptuously rejects the tradition, vouched for (he says) by no reputable source, that Tiberius, dinner guest of his son, passed to Drusus the poisoned cup which he had been warned Drusus would offer him.[53] When Drusus went to Illyricum with proconsular power, Tacitus gives as one of the Em-

---

[50] Dio, 57. 22. 3; Tac., 2. 43. 6; Suet., 52. 1.
[51] Dio, 57. 13. 1 f.   [52] Tac., 1. 76. 5, 7.   [53] *Id.*, 4. 10. 1-11. 3.

peror's motives for the appointment the desire to get his son away from his lascivious life in the capital to the military discipline of the camp;[54] and, while we may consider that reasons of State rather determined the appointment, we need not deny that Tiberius might welcome the opportunity to change the environment of Drusus' life. We may add, finally, the triviality, supplied by the elder Pliny, that Drusus in accord with the views of the epicure Apicius, disdained the young shoots of cabbage, for which Tiberius criticized him.[55]

Of relations with his own children we have not a word beyond the probably politic statement in the Senate already referred to.[56]

[54] *Id.*, 2. 44. 1.   [55] *N. H.*, 19. 137.

[56] We know the names of numerous slaves and freedmen of the family: *C. I. L.*, VI, 4337 (= Dess., 1718), Bassus Germanus, slave of Drusus, formerly of Germanicus.

VI, 8848, Antigonus, Drusus' slave poulterer.

VI, 20237 (= Dess., 8052), Prosopa, freedman of Julia Augusta, but favorite of Livilla, as of the dowager empress.

VI, 33787 (= Dess., 1828), Prytanis, freedman of Augusta, but *paedagogus* of Livilla.

VI, 4349 (= Dess., 1751), Olympus, Livilla's *lecticarius*.

VI, 5198 (= Dess., 1752), Antiochus, her *supra lecticarios*.

VI, 19747, Iucundus, Livilla's slave.

VI, 8899 (= Dess., 1843), Cyrus, Livilla's physician.

VI, 5226, Ti. Claudius Alexander, Livilla's freedman, and Claudia Libas, her freedwoman.

VI, 15502 (= Dess., 8054), Claudia Melpomene, Livilla's freedwoman.

VI, 38204, Claudia Storge, Livilla's freedwoman.

VI, 4119, Elate, Julia's freedwoman.

VI, 9095, Thullius Castor, attendant upon Gemellus.

Pliny, *N. H.*, 29. 20; Tac., 4. 3. 5; 4. 11. 4, name another physician of Livilla, Eudemus; and Tac., 4. 10. 2; 4. 11. 4, mentions Lygdus, Drusus' eunuch and, probably, *praegustator*. *I. G. R. R.*, IV, 219 (at Ilium) honors a φροντιστής (*procurator*) of Drusus, Titus Valerius Proculus, for his suppression of piracy.

Whether Amethystus Drusi Caesar (is), who had a house below the Pincian Hill, *C. I. L.*, XV, 7383, Platner-Ashby, *op. cit.*, 155, was the slave (or freedman) of our Drusus or of Germanicus' son Drusus, is doubtful.

II. DRUSUS' PUBLIC CAREER

The group of inscriptions (and statues, no doubt, though they are not extant) set up in A.D. 7-8 at Ticinum in honor of Augustus and his family [1] shows Drusus' position in that family after the adoptions of A.D. 4. The order of persons on one side of Augustus' central figure is Tiberius, Germanicus, Drusus and Germanicus' son, Nero. And Drusus is described as *Drusus Julius Ti.f.Augusti nepos divi pronepos Caesar pontifex.*

The pontificate, which appears also on coins of Drusus and in other inscriptions,[2] seems to have been his earliest official honor. On 14 May, A.D. 14 Drusus was co-opted as a *Frater Arvalis* to fill the vacancy left by the untimely death of Lucius Aemilius Paullus, the son of Agrippa's daughter Julia.[3] We know that he was present at the meeting of the Brothers 15 December that year, at which were co-opted two new members of the priesthood, Gnaeus Pompeius, the augur, in the place, apparently, of Gnaeus Pompeius, the suffect consul of 31 B.C., and, to succeed Augustus, some unidentified person whose name was subsequently erased because of *damnatio memoriae.*[4] And another fragment of the *acta Arvalium* records his attendance early in the year 21.[5] Some time in the last months of A.D. 14, a new priesthood was created, the *Sodales Augustales*, to the

---

[1] Dess., 107 (= *C.I.L.*, V, 6416).

[2] *B.M.C.*, Tib., 95-97, 99-101; Dess., 168 (= *C.I.L.*, VI, 910); Dess., 169 (= *C.I.L.*, XII, 147); *C.I.L.*, II, 2040, 2338; VI, 31280; X, 4573, 4617, 4638; XI, 4777; XIII, 1036, 5199; XIV, 5322 (before A.D. 11).

[3] Dess., 5026 (= *C.I.L.*, VI, 2023, cf. 36907, on which Huelsen in *Klio*, 2 [1902], 240 and Groag, in *Prosop.*², A, 392).

[4] Dess., *loc. cit.*   [5] *Ibid.*

honor and cult of the now deified Augustus. After the selection by lot of twenty-one *primores civitatis*, four additional members were named, seemingly by the Senate, Tiberius, Drusus, Germanicus and Claudius, to compose the new college.[6] Drusus also became augur and *flamen Augustalis*, probably after Germanicus' death, and *quindecimvir*.[7] When the dowager empress Livia recovered from an illness in 22 the Senate decreed sacrifices to the gods, and games over which pontiffs, augurs, *quindecimviri, septemviri* and *Sodales Augustales* should preside; Drusus as a member of four out of the five colleges concerned, was doubtless present at that function.[8]

It is noticeable that at Ticinum neither Germanicus nor Drusus is named *princeps iuventutis*. Yet by A. D. 9, if not before, they had been so designated, for Ovid, writing in that year, applies to them the phrase *sidus iuvenale*,[9] clear indication of their identification with Castor and Pollux, an identification regularly associated with the *principatus iuventutis*.[10] There is abundant

[6] Tac., 1. 54. 1 f.; cf. *C. I. L.*, V, 4954; VI, 910; IX, 35; X, 4638; XI, 3787.
[7] Augur: Dess., 168 (= *C. I. L.*, VI, 910); 169 (= *C. I. L.*, XII, 147) (both dated A. D. 23 or later); *C. I. L.*, IX, 35 (clearly after A. D. 14, and its plausible restoration dates it A. D. 23 or later); XIII, 1036 (after Germanicus' death). Flamen: Dess., 169 (= *C. I. L.*, XII, 147); Dessau, *ad loc.*, considers *flamen* an error for *sodalis*, but advances no reason. Germanicus had been both augur and *flamen Augustalis*; after his decease the Senate decreed that only a member of the Julian house might succeed him in those priesthoods, Tac., 2. 83. 2. Furneaux, *ad Tac., loc. cit.*, thought Drusus was that successor; surely, no one else was so likely. Quindecimvir: *C. I. L.*, V, 4954; Dessau, *loc. cit.*, has some doubts about the restoration of this inscription, but the *Corpus* gives XV VI and half of an R as showing on the stone.
[8] Tac., 3. 64. 3.
[9] *Trist.*, 2. 167; on the poem's date cf. Schanz-Hosius, 245.
[10] K. Scott in *C. P.*, 25 (1930), 158-161; Weinstock in *Studi e Materiali d. Storia d. Religioni*, 12 (1937), 20-23.

further evidence of this cult of Germanicus and Drusus as the Dioscuri. They had a *flamen* at Nimes; and they appear together in their divine character in inscriptions at Patara in Lycia, at Olympia and on coins.[11]

Drusus' political career was several times accelerated in its early years. When the title of *Imperator* was conferred upon Augustus and Tiberius, and *ornamenta triumphalia* granted to Germanicus at the victorious suppression of the Pannonian mutiny in A. D. 9, certain privileges were voted also to Drusus, according to Dio, "although he had taken no part in the war." [12] One doubts then, that the Senate's decree regarding Drusus had any other connection with those celebrating the conclusion of the war, than chance coincidence of date. It was, at all events, provided that Drusus might attend meetings of the Senate, in spite of having held no magistracy, presumably, therefore, as auditor only, and that, on entering its membership when he should have held the quaestorship, he should rank at the head of the ex-praetors. Two years later he served as quaestor,[13] but what quaestorian function he filled we do not know. In A. D. 12 Drusus marched in Tiberius' triumph with

[11] *C. I. L.*, XII, 3180, 3207; *I. G. R. R.*, III, 680; *Inscr. Olymp.*, 372; *B. M. C.*, *Lydia*, Sardes 104-109, cf. 110-112; *B. M. C.*, *Caria*, Tabae 61, 62; cf. *B. M. C.*, *Phrygia*, Hierapolis, 111; *C. A. H.*, *Plates* V, 200 q.; Ovid, *Pont.*, 2. 2. 83 ff.; 2. 5. 41. Balsdon has cited the silence of the *monumentum Ancyranum* and the absence of the title from inscriptions of Germanicus and Drusus as indications that the title was not conferred on either of them, *J. R. S.*, 26 (1936), 156 and cf. Gagé, *R. E. A.*, 37 (1935), 171 f. But the former is by no means surprising since there was little revision of the *Res Gestae* so late; and the latter is certainly not conclusive as against the evidence afforded by Ovid, the cult of the brothers as the *Dioscuri*, and the mention of the shield in *C. I. L.*, VI, 31200, cf. *infra*, 133.

[12] Dio, 56. 17. 3; cf. *C. I. L.*, VI, 31194.

[13] Dio, 56. 25. 4; cf. *C. I. L.*, XII, 147.

Germanicus, Messalinus and Cotta Maximus;[14] and the next year his praetorian rank was confirmed when Augustus authorized his standing for the consulship of 15 without having passed through the praetorship.[15] It is erroneous to say, as some modern writers do,[16] that Tiberius gave his son the first consulship at his disposal; Drusus was consul-designate before Augustus died.[17] In the same year Augustus arranged the constitution of a *consilium* whose resolutions should have equal validity with the decisions of the whole Senate.[18] The *consilium* was to consist of twenty senators appointed annually, with the addition of the consuls and the consuls-designate *ex officio*, Tiberius, whose tribunician power was now renewed, and the Emperor's grandchildren, Germanicus and Drusus.

Immediately following his account of this council Dio sets down Augustus' reply to the vehement agitation against the five percent tax on inheritances. The Emperor intimated that the Senate might investigate the problem and submit to him proposals for alternative measures to produce an equivalent revenue. At the same time he forbade Germanicus and Drusus to enter actively into the discussions, anticipating that any statement by them would be interpreted as prompted by him.[19] Here again is clear indication of Drusus' increasing significance in the political field.

[14] Ovid, *Pont.*, 2. 2. 81 ff.
[15] Dio, 56. 28. 1.
[16] Gardthausen in P. W., X, 432: Charlesworth in *C. A. H.*, X, 624; Ciaceri, *Tiberio Successore di Augusto*, 109.
[17] Hohl also has noticed this: *Klio*, 30 (1937), 332, n. 1.
[18] Dio, 56. 28. 2 f.; cf. M. Hammond, *The Augustan Principate*, 168.
[19] Dio, 56.28. 4 f.

In the obsequies of Augustus Drusus figured pro-
minently. At the first meeting of the Senate convoked
by Tiberius,[20] Tiberius commenced a prepared speech,
but was unable because of his grief to continue speaking,
and delivered the text to Drusus who read the balance
of this address to the House.[21] Both wore mourning
on this occasion.[22] The late Emperor's will, brought by
Drusus from the Vestal Virgins who had been its cus-
todians, was read: it named Tiberius as heir to two-
thirds of the estate, Livia to the remaining one-third;
as heirs in default Drusus to receive one-third, Germanicus and his three sons the other two-thirds.[23] On
the funeral day, Augustus' coffin enclosed in a gold and
ivory couch draped with purple and gold was borne
along in the procession. A waxen image in triumphal
robes was carried by the magistrates-designate, among
whom Drusus was, of course, numbered. The procession
halted at the old rostra, where Drusus delivered an
eulogy of a personal and private character. There followed another halt before the temple of Divus Iulius
where the eulogy for the State was spoken by Tiberius.
Then the cortège, images and bier, magistrates, senators,
knights and their wives, and military escort, moved on
to the Campus Martius where priests, citizens and
soldiery paid the last honors and Augustus' body was
cremated.[24]

---

[20] Tac., 1. 7. 5 f.   [21] Suet., 23.   [22] Dio, 56. 31. 3.

[23] Tac., 1. 8. 1 f.; Suet., *Aug.*, 101. 1 f.; Dio, 56. 32. 1 a, 1. For full and
detailed discussion of the proceedings of the Senate between Augustus'
death and the formal accession of Tiberius, cf. E. Hohl, in *Hermes*, 68
(1933), 106-115, and in *Klio*, 30 (1937), 323-328, 332 and notes 4 and 6.
Hohl has shown that Drusus read only Tiberius' address, and not the
various documents left by Augustus as well.

[24] Dio, 56. 34-42; Suet., *Aug.*, 100. 3.

At the meeting of the Senate on 17 September [25]
Tiberius asked the proconsular imperium for Germanicus, but not for Drusus, we are told, " quod desig-
natus consul Drusus praesensque erat." [26] Within the
next day or two Drusus departed from Rome, dispatched by Tiberius to deal with the Pannonian mutiny,[27] presumably as *legatus Augusti*. He was not
bound by fixed instructions but was to use his best
judgment on the spot. The mutiny had broken out on
receipt of the news of Augustus' death in the summer
quarters of the three legions, VIII Augusta, IX Hispana
and XV Apollinaris, which formed the command of
Quintus Junius Blaesus, the governor of Pannonia.
Blaesus had of course suspended routine activity in
observance of the *iustitium*. The soldiers, idle and rest-
less, listened to the agitation of Percennius and others,
and demanded increased pay, shorter term of service,
and cash- (not land-) bonus on discharge. Blaesus,
appealing for the maintenance of discipline, urged that
they appoint spokesmen to present their demands to
him. They so appointed the younger Blaesus, the
legate's son, and agitation subsided temporarily. Meantime detachments of the legions on duty at Nauportus,
mutinied, plundered that town and nearby villages,
abused Aufidienus Rufus, the *praefectus castrorum*, and
returned to the summer camp to join their comrades,
whereupon the mutiny again broke out. Blaesus flogged
and imprisoned a few offenders. Their comrades then
burst open the camp prison and released all its inmates.

[25] Cf. E. Hohl in *Hermes*, 68 (1933), 110-115.
[26] Tac., 1. 14. 4 f.
[27] Hohl, *loc. cit.*, 107; Tac., 1. 24. 1.

More leaders arose, including a private soldier, Vibulenus, and discipline was completely overthrown; tribunes
and prefect were driven out of camp and a centurion
murdered. Then VIII Augusta and XV Apollinaris
quarrelled with each other and only the efforts of IX
Hispana kept them from fighting.[28]

As news of Augustus' death reached the troops before
they mutinied, the uprising can be dated to the very
end of August or the opening days of September. For
a time Blaesus seems to have been able to consider that
he had the situation in hand, and he may not have
reported to Rome until after the second outbreak. News
would then reach Rome about mid-September.[29]

Drusus was given a staff made up of *primores civitatis,* and an escort of troops, consisting of two praetorian cohorts augmented by soldiers from the other
cohorts of the Guard, together with a large part of the
praetorian cavalry and most of the imperial bodyguard
of Germans. In command of these troops went Lucius
Aelius Sejanus, the colleague of his father, Lucius Aelius
Strabo, in the Prefecture of the Guard. His regular
command seems to have been the reason for his receiving this assignment, but it may be noted in addition that
he was a nephew of Blaesus the governor. Sejanus was
to be " rector " to Drusus.[30] This is the first occasion on
which they were associated, so far as we know; they
were to be linked together the rest of Drusus' life.[31] Of
other members of Drusus' staff we learn the names of

[28] Tac., 1. 16-23.

[29] Hohl, *loc. cit.*, 107, reckons nine or ten days from Rome to Nauportus,
and believes Tiberius did not delay between receipt of the news and dispatching Drusus.

[30] Tac., 1. 24. 1-3.   [31] *V. infra*, ch. 3.

two: Gnaeus Cornelius Lentulus and Lucius Aponius.[32] The former we cannot positively identify. Tacitus says of him, " ante alios aetate et gloria belli." This service with Drusus and the conquest of the Dacians,[33] are referred tentatively by Groag[33a] to Lentulus Augur, consul in 14 B. C. Aponius was a Roman knight, perhaps the same person whose equestrian career, ending with the prefecture of Gaius Caesar's duovirate of Baeterrae (Béziers) in the Narbonese province, is recorded by an inscription.[34]

Drusus reached the legionary camp in Pannonia evidently on 26 September.[35] The troops were surly, and admitted with Drusus into the camp only a part of his escort, forcing the rest to remain outside and making fast the camp gates against them. Before a moody and turbulent assemblage Drusus read the dispatch which he bore from Tiberius. The message was to the effect that the legions with which he had so often campaigned were Tiberius' foremost concern: that, as soon as he recovered from his grief at Augustus' death, he would take up their demands with the Senate; that meantime Drusus would immediately concede them what could be granted at once; and that the rest must be reserved to the Senate which should be regarded as competent to grant or refuse. The assembly said that the centurion Clemens would speak for it. Clemens put the demands of discharge after sixteen (instead of twenty) years, pay of a denarius (instead of ten *asses*) per day, and

---

[32] Tac., 1. 27. 1; 1. 29. 2.
[33] Dated between A. D. 1 and 4 by Syme in *J. R. S.*, 24 (1934), 113-137.
[33a] *Prosop.*[2], C, 1379; but cf. #1378, the consul of 18 B. C.
[34] *C. I. L.*, XII, 4230; cf. 4235. Cf. Stein in *Prosop.*[2], A, 934.
[35] Cf. *infra*.

that veterans be not retained on vexillary duty after discharge from regular service. Drusus said the Senate and Tiberius must rule on those proposals, and was howled down—why had he come if he had no authority to speak? They refused to listen further, assumed a threatening attitude toward any praetorian or member of Drusus' suite whom they encountered, and most especially toward Lentulus. He therefore left the camp for the security of the winter quarters, but not without being stoned and wounded before he escaped out the gate to the protection of Drusus' troops outside.

The night which followed, 26/27 September, was marked by an eclipse of the moon,[36] a phenomenon which worked mightily on the superstitious natures of the soldiers. Drusus won Clemens and others who were in the soldiers' confidence, and by their persuasion the legions were recalled to discipline. On the next day Drusus again addressed an assembly, without gift of rhetoric but with innate dignity. He reprehended their former, approved their latter actions, said he was unmoved by intimidation or threats, but if he saw and heard evidence of their return to obedience, would ask Tiberius to listen to their petitions. The assembly designated young Blaesus, Aponius, and Catonius Justus, a high-ranking centurion [37] to convey their petitions to Tiberius. There followed debate whether the return of these representatives should be awaited or penalty visited at once upon the instigators of the mutiny. Tacitus says: "promptum ad asperiora Drusi

---

[36] Lunar eclipse #1884 in Th. v. Oppolzer, *Canon der Finsternisse*, p. 343. The eclipse was total about dawn as the moon was near its setting.

[37] Praetorian prefect under Claudius, *Prosop.*[2], C, 576.

ingenium erat." He summoned Vibulenus and Percennius and had them summarily executed. Tacitus reports that most authors recorded that their bodies were hastily buried within Drusus' quarters, others that they were thrown outside the rampart as an object lesson. The latter version seems rather more in Drusus' character; he had shown no disposition to shirk responsibility for any action of his.

Other ring-leaders were then hunted down by centurions and praetorians outside the camp or their own comrades within, and done to death. Torrential rains of a very early winter were, like the eclipse, superstitiously interpreted as signs of heaven's wrath. The eighth legion went off to its winter quarters; the fifteenth followed. The ninth wanted to wait for Tiberius' answer, but, deserted by the other two, itself also repaired to winter camp. Drusus returned forthwith to Rome.[38] He was then, presumably, in Rome again before mid-October.

When Tiberius reported to the Senate the suppression of the mutinies in Germany and Pannonia, he spoke, we are told, more briefly but more sincerely of Drusus' work than of Germanicus' measures in Germany.[39] This is ascribed to his suspicions and jealousy of Germanicus and Agrippina. I have indicated elsewhere [40] my belief that such suspicions, as regards Agrippina, were well-grounded. But sufficient reason for the different atti-

---

[38] Tac., 1. 24-30. Other sources for the mutiny, which however add nothing to Tacitus, are Dio, 57. 4; Vell., 2. 125. 4 f. and Suet., 25. 1 f. Suetonius gives the pay increase demanded as the equivalent of the praetorians' stipend, erroneously it seems.

[39] Tac., 1. 52. 3; cf. Dio, 57. 6. 4.

[40] *T. A. P. A.*, 62 (1931), 149-151; cf. especially Tac., 1. 69.

tude toward Drusus, if reason must be assigned, is the more competent, more straightforward conduct of Drusus as contrasted with the cowardly refusal of responsibility and the contemptible forging of a letter from Tiberius, which had been the features of Germanicus' actions. Drusus had been heavy-handed, not to say brutal, but courageous and firm, not weak and yielding. Sacrifices in honor of the achievements of both were proposed by Tiberius, according to Dio.[41] In the ensuing winter Ovid wrote, in reference to Germanicus and Drusus:

> duos iuvenes, firma adiumenta parentis,
> qui dederint animi pignora certa sui.[42]

Early in A.D. 15, probably between 10 March and 27 June, is dated the Gytheate decree instituting the *Caesarea* in honor of the imperial family as it was constituted after Augustus' death.[43] The fifth day of the *Caesarea* was devoted to "the Aphrodite of Drusus Caesar." This rather curious phrase has been convincingly interpreted by Rostovtzeff.[44] Citing the worship of Livilla at Ilium as θεὰ ᾿Αφροδείτη ᾿Αγχεισιάς [45]—who is certainly to be identified with Venus Genetrix—and the appearance of Julian as well as Claudian *imagines* in the funeral procession of Drusus,[46] he rightly finds evidence of an endeavor to buttress the political position of Drusus by emphasizing his connection through his

[41] *Loc. cit.*
[42] *Pont.*, 4.13.31 f.; cf. Schanz-Hosius, 247.
[43] Cf. especially H. Seyrig in *Rev. Arch.*, XXIX (1929), 84-106; E. Kornemann, *Neue Dokumente zum lakonischen Kaiserkult*, and M. Rostovtzeff in *Rev. Hist.*, 163 (1930), 1-26; for the date, L. R. Taylor, *T.A.P.A.*, 60 (1929), 89, n. 7.
[44] *Loc. cit.*, 18.   [45] Dess., 8787.   [46] Tac., 4.9.3.

wife with the Julian line. We know from a statement of
Tacitus, writing of the year 17, that there were in the
city of Rome a party of Germanicus and a party of
Drusus, and that Tiberius favored Drusus out of affection for the son of his own blood.[47] Whatever may have
been the composition of the group, it is evident that
there were in the early years of Tiberius' reign persons
who believed that either by natural affection for his own
son, or by some political pressure, Tiberius might be
induced to overthrow the arrangement of Augustus,
which made Germanicus the preferred successor to the
imperial position.[48] The inscriptions of Ilium and Gy-
theum show that the party of Drusus was not restricted
to the capital city. We know that Agrippina made
special boast of her direct descent from Augustus;[49] it
was inevitable that the rival party should set up its claim
to relationship with the Divus.[50] Drusus had passed
into the Julian *gens,* equally with Germanicus, through
Tiberius' adoption by Augustus. And Livilla was the
granddaughter of Augustus' sister, Octavia; also she
was, "in fact if not in law" (as Rostovtzeff puts it),
doubly member of Augustus' family by reason of her
marriages to Gaius Caesar and to Drusus.

With the commencement of A. D. 15 Drusus entered
upon the consulship to which Augustus had designated
him, having as his colleague Gaius Norbanus Flaccus,

[47] Tac., 2. 43. 5-7. These parties have been discussed by Marsh in
A. H. R., 31 (1925/6), 233-250; cf. *id., The Reign of Tiberius,* index, *s. v.*
Drusus, party of. His conclusions are not accepted by R. Syme, *The
Roman Revolution,* 434, n. 5. Cf. also now W. Allen in *T. A. P. A.,* 72
(1941), 1-25.
[48] Marsh, *op. cit.,* 68, n. 1.
[49] Tac., 1. 40. 3; 4. 52. 4. Cf. *T. A. P. A.,* 62 (1931), 154.
[50] Cf. Gagé, "Divus Augustus," in *Rev. Arch.,* 34 (1931), 11-41.

son perhaps of Augustus' colleague in 23 B. C.[51] Drusus continued in office throughout the year; Flaccus was succeeded, doubtless on 1 July, by Marcus Junius Silanus, who enjoyed the high respect of Tiberius and was later to become the father-in-law of Gaius.[52] Dio remarks that Drusus performed the consular functions just as anyone else would have done; [53] he is not mentioned by name in the activities of the consuls recorded in the historians' account of the year. But before the consuls came the indictments for *maiestas* of Faianius and Rubrius, and of Granius Marcellus. All were quashed by Tiberius, the first two at once, the other as trial was about to commence in the Senate.[54] In the course of the year the Senate debated the appeal of Aurelius Pius for indemnification for the damage done his house by the building of a street and an aqueduct; [55] the request of Propertius Celer to withdraw from the order because of poverty; [56] the problem of floods of the Tiber; [57] the transfer from senatorial to imperial administration of Achaea and Macedonia in response to their petition for abatement of taxation; [58] the riotous disorderliness of the acting profession which had resulted in several fatalities; [59] and the petition of Hither Spain to erect a temple to Augustus in Tarraco.[60]

---

[51] Tac., 1. 55. 1; *Prosop.*, N, 137; cf. Dio, 57. 14. 1; Dess., 167 (= *C. I. L.*, II, 3829); *Fasti, C. I. L.*, I², pp. 74, 233, 242; also *C. I. L.*, I, 761; IV, 5214; VI, 10051 (= Dess., 5283); 37836 (= Dess., 9349); X, 3786, 6639; Suet., *Vit.*, 3. 2.

[52] *Prosop.*, I, 551; *C. I. L.*, X, 6639; I, 762 (dated 13 August), 763. Flaccus was still in office 13 June, *C. I. L.*, I, 761.

[53] Dio, 57. 14. 9.

[54] Full discussion and citation of evidence in my *Criminal Trials*, 8-10.

[55] Tac., 1. 75. 3 f.; cf. *supra*, 10.

[56] Tac., 1. 75. 5; cf. *supra*, 6.

[57] Tac., 1. 76. 1; 1. 79; Dio, 57. 14. 7 f.

[58] Tac., 1. 76. 4; 1. 80. 1.

[59] Tac., 1. 77; cf. Dio, 57. 14. 10.

[60] Tac., 1. 78. 1.

Of Drusus' other activities in the year we know a little. He presided at a gladiatorial spectacle produced in his own and Germanicus' name, and manifested an obvious and excessive enjoyment of the blood-letting. Tiberius was said to have censured him for this conduct, as tending to alarm the populace.[61] His intimacy with the actors is alleged by Dio to have been the cause of their rioting, though Tacitus does not name him in this connection. Nor is such a relation entirely implausible; it would be quite in character for Drusus to associate with the capital's low-life, and the actors might expect the favor of the Emperor's son to furnish impunity for their unlicensed conduct.[62]

The following year, A. D. 16, Drusus remained in Rome. Marsh has pointed out the significance of this circumstance to the maturing of the conspiracy of Libo Drusus.[63] Tiberius, Germanicus and Drusus were all in Rome, accessible to assassination in 16. Libo's plot had been formed immediately after Tiberius' accession; between its inception and its denunciation and suppression, the Emperor had taken precautions against any attempt at assassination by the known conspirator, including Drusus' presence at any interview between Tiberius and Libo.[64] There can be no doubt that Libo's plot was what the *Fasti Amiternini* represented it— " nefaria consilia . . . de salute Ti. Caesaris liberorum-

[61] Tac., 1. 76. 5-7; cf. Dio, 57. 14. 3. Tacitus' words can equally be interpreted that " Drusus' conduct was alarming to the populace and Tiberius was said to have censured him."

[62] Dio, 57. 14. 10; cf. *infra*, 150, 152.

[63] *Reign of Tiberius*, 58 f.; C. P., 21 (1926), 298 f. For a full account of the trial of Libo with references to the sources, cf. my *Criminal Trials*, 12-20.

[64] Suet., 25. 3.

que eius et aliorum principum civitatis deque re publica." For although the *Fasti* represent, of course, an official version of the episode, they are corroborated, not only by Velleius (also official, presumably), but by Seneca, Suetonius and Dio, and only Tacitus disagrees. Marsh has convincingly referred the Tacitean version to propaganda of the Scribonian family.[65] Libo committed suicide in anticipation of conviction. Thus Drusus escaped an attempt upon his life.

In seeming consequence of the trial of Libo there was a senatorial investigation of astrologers. Drusus figured in the debate on penalties to be imposed for persistence in the practice of astrology. Together with the Emperor he proposed for citizens convicted on the charge confiscation of property and banishment. Gnaeus Piso countered with a motion that no punishment be inflicted on citizens. The Senate voted the latter motion, only to have it vetoed by a tribune (under instructions from Tiberius?). Evidently the prior motion was then voted into law.[66]

Shortly after Germanicus was appointed in A. D. 17 with proconsular imperium to administer the Eastern provinces and arrange a settlement with Parthia of the Armenian problem, Drusus received a rather similar commission in Illyricum. Civil war had broken out in Germany after the withdrawal of Germanicus from the Rhine the year before. Arminius led a coalition of Cherusci with the Semnones and Langobardi who had revolted from Maroboduus; opposed to him was Maro-

[65] *C. P.*, 21 (1926), 300 f.
[66] Tac., 2. 32. 5; Dio, 57. 15. 8 f.; cf. *C. P.*, 26 (1931), 203 f., and *Criminal Trials*, 20 f.

boduus, supported by Arminius' uncle Inguiomerus and the latter's clients, at the head of the remaining Suebic peoples. Maroboduus, defeated in battle, had taken refuge among the Marcomanni and appealed to Tiberius for aid. Tiberius denied the request on the ground that when the Romans had been at war with the Cherusci, they had received no aid from Maroboduus.

Tacitus represents this appeal as the pretext merely of Drusus' appointment to Illyricum, assigning as the real reasons that Tiberius wished to separate his son from his luxurious life in the capital and subject him to the more wholesome influence of military discipline, and that he desired to have both his sons in command of legionary armies in the interest of his own security. The historian, however, contradicts himself by saying later that Drusus was sent to be " paci firmator." We may accept the German situation, which required watching, and the need of maintaining peace and order in neighboring Illyricum as the genuine and principal reason for Drusus' despatch east of the Adriatic, without denying that the other ends were regarded by Tiberius as desirable.[67]

Because of Tacitus' topical arrangement of material within the limits of each year,[68] we cannot know whether Drusus was still in Rome to be present at the trial of Appuleia Varilla on charges of *maiestas* and adultery, or to hear the report of Camillus' progress in the war against Tacfarinas.[69] But we are specifically informed that, before leaving the capital, Drusus joined Germanicus in supporting the candidacy of Decimus

[67] Tac., 2. 44-46.
[68] F. A. Marx, in *Hermes*, 60 (1925), 74-93.
[69] Tac., 2. 50; 2. 52. 9.

Haterius Agrippa (a distant relative of Germanicus) to succeed Vipstanus Gallus, deceased in his praetorship. Evidently there was another candidate in close competition with Agrippa, for we hear that many senators favored the invocation of the Lex Papia Poppaea, which provided that, of two candidates for office receiving an equal number of votes, the one having the larger number of children was to be elected. Says Tacitus: "Laetabatur Tiberius, cum inter filios eius et leges senatus disceptaret." The sentence is very easy to misinterpret, prejudices against Tiberius and preconceptions about his government being what they are. The following rendering [70] represents what is probably a rather common understanding: "Tiberius was overjoyed to see the senate divided between his sons and the laws." That is perhaps what the hostile critic of Tiberius would wish Tacitus to have said, but it is not what Tacitus did say. "Tiberius was glad that the Senate was deciding an issue between his sons and the laws." Evidence has been cited [71] that Tiberius was consistently and earnestly concerned that the Senate should accept responsibility and assume a share in the tasks of administration. Also he considered that no special prerogatives belonged to the members of his family.[72] Germanicus and Drusus, on the contrary, evidently believed that, as the Emperor's sons, they were entitled to have their own way in this matter of Agrippa's election. It was a hopeful sign, from Tiberius' point of view, that the Senate had gathered enough courage to decide the issue. At that he rejoiced. Tacitus con-

---

[70] By John Jackson in the Loeb Library.
[71] Supra, 78 ff.   [72] Supra, 70 ff.

tinues: "Victa est sine dubio lex, sed neque statim et paucis suffragiis, quo modo etiam cum valerent, leges vincebantur."[73] Tiberius said nothing; it was his custom, sometimes unfortunate, not to speak, and on this occasion, any comment, of course, could only have been in conflict with his own policy that the Senate should take responsible action. The whole incident is most illuminating on the characters of Tiberius and his sons, and of his policy.

Well before the end of 17 Drusus, evidently accompanied by Livilla,[74] set out for Illyricum. For Germanicus, *en route* to the East, visited his brother in Delmatia, and was himself in Nicopolis to enter there upon his consulship on 1 January, 18. The legionary camps in Delmatia seem to have been Burnum and Gardun; we can probably assume that Drusus was in one or the other of those places when his brother visited him.[75] His command in Illyricum he held until A. D. 20, although he was not continuously in his province.

We have now to ask what his province was and what was the nature of his command. Our sources give the following indications on the former question.

Drusus in Illyricum missus est.
missus . . . Drusus . . . paci firmator.
Germanicus . . . viso fratre Druso in Delmatia agente.
Drusus Illyricos ad exercitus profectus.
Drusus rediens Illyrico.
Drusus (Caesar) triumphavit ex Ill (yrico).[76]

[73] Tac., 2. 51.
[74] Id., 3. 34. 13.
[75] Id., 2. 53. 1; Parker, The Roman Legions, 123; Syme in C. A. H., X, 804 and n. 1.
[76] Tac., 2. 44. 1; 2. 46. 6; 2. 53. 1; 3. 7. 1; 3. 11. 1; C. I. L., XIV, 244.

Evidently Drusus' province was designated officially as Illyricum. But the name Illyricum at this period described a group of provinces, *viz.*, Upper Illyricum, later called Delmatia, Lower Illyricum, i. e., Pannonia, and Upper Moesia; and it was employed sometimes in a still wider sense to include also Raetia, Noricum and Dacia.[77] Drusus was commissioned to protect the peace of Roman territories from disturbance by the struggle of the neighboring Germans. That strife centered in Bohemia, bordering on Raetia and Noricum. And to Noricum Maroboduus fled after his defeat. The *regnum Vannianum* which Drusus constituted was across the Danube from Pannonia. And Tacitus specifically mentions Drusus' presence in Delmatia. Probably, therefore, at the very least, Delmatia, Pannonia, Noricum and Raetia were comprised in Drusus' command.

And the command was an *imperium maius*. For Publius Cornelius Dolabella continued as governor of Delmatia; inscriptions which show him holding that commission can be dated in A. D. 14, 16/17, 18/19, and 19/20.[78] Whether Quintus Junius Blaesus, governor of Pannonia in 14, was still there, we do not know. He was in Rome in 21, but so too was Dolabella then.[79] In Raetia and Noricum were procurators whose names are not known. The army of Pannonia consisted of the three legions, VIII Augusta, IX Hispana and XV Apollinaris. In Delmatia were the VII and XI, both of

---

[77] Cf. Vulić in P. W., IX, 1087 and references there.

[78] *C. I. L.*, III, 1741 (= Dess., 938) in A. D. 14; 3198 (= 10156 = Dess., 5829) in 16/17; 3199 (= 10157) before 18; 2908 (= Dess., 2280) in 18/19; 3201 (= 10159 = Dess., 5829a) in 19/20; cf. 3200 (= 10158), 14712.

[79] Tac., 3. 35; 3. 47. 4.

which later bore the name Claudia.[80] The auxiliary troops in the four provinces we cannot identify.

Our sources provide little enough detail on Drusus' administration of his province. The year 18 he spent endeavoring to nurture the disharmony among the Germans and bring about the complete overthrow of the now weakened Maroboduus.[81] Catualda, a Suebic noble who had fled from Maroboduus' kingdom and found refuge among the Gotones, now returned, perhaps at Tiberius' instigation, with a strong following, won adherents among the Marcomannic nobles and successfully attacked Maroboduus' palace and capital. Maroboduus crossed the Danube in flight to Noricum and petitioned Tiberius for asylum, claiming it as due reward for old friendship. Tiberius acceded and the exile was domiciled at Ravenna, free to return to Germany whenever he wished and potentially useful to Tiberius who could threaten his restoration to his throne if the Suebi became unruly.[82] This internment of Maroboduus Tiberius reported to the Senate in an address which was still extant in Tacitus' time. With some extravagance, perhaps, the Emperor compared the menace of Maroboduus to that of Philip to Athens or of Pyrrhus and Antiochus to Rome. But it was with complete justifica-

[80] Tac., 1. 23. 6; Ritterling in P. W., XII, 1617, 1691.

[81] Tac., 2. 62. I accept Steup's transposition of chapters 62-67 to follow 58 (Rh. M., 24 [1869], 72-80). The objection of Stein (P. W., XIV, 1910) does not disturb me. It is better to suppose A. D. 19 inactive and the ovatio of 20 delayed (v. infra, 123), than that Drusus failed to take advantage of conditions in Germany and remained inert during the first year of his command. In view of the exiguity of our sources, we cannot too confidently restrict to one year the recorded activity of Drusus. And finally Steup has positive and cogent arguments for the transposition, which are hardly impaired by the negative objection of Stein.

[82] Tac., 2. 62 f.; Vell., 2. 129. 3; Suet., 37. 4; cf. Stein, loc. cit.

tion that he rehearsed the great power which Maroboduus had held, the ferocity of his subjects and the threat
to Italy implicit in the geographical location of that
power. Finally he narrated the details of the policy by
which he had wrought Maroboduus' downfall.[83] Catualda fared no better. The Hermunduri drove him out
of Bohemia; he too sought Roman asylum and was
allowed to reside at Forum Iulii.[84] The clients of Maroboduus and Catualda, evidently numerous, were not,
however, admitted within the Empire's boundaries for
fear of disturbance in the provinces. They were settled
on land along the left bank of the Danube between the
rivers Marus and Cusus (the March and, probably, the
Waag).[85] And Drusus set up the Quadian Vannius as
king of the Marcomanni and the Quadi; thus was constituted the so-called *regnum Vannianum*, a client state
of Rome.[87]

The degree of Drusus' success and the significance
of his achievement are best gauged by the fact that
" another fifty years were to pass before Rome ex-
perienced any serious trouble from German tribes."[87]
But Dessau is contemptuous of Drusus' accomplish-
ment. First, it was diplomatic, not military; second,
the credit was Tiberius' not Drusus'; and third, Dessau
sneers that perhaps Drusus never left Delmatia for the
Danube frontier.[88] Since Drusus was specifically commissioned as " paci firmator,"[89] and we are told that

---

[83] Tac., 2. 63. 3 f.   [84] *Id.*, 2. 63. 6.
[85] *Id.*, 2. 63. 7; cf. Schmidt in *Hermes*, 48 (1913), 292; Schwarz in
Sudeta, 8 (1931), 145 and in *Forsch. u. Fortschr.*, 9 (1933), 35.
[86] Tac., *loc. cit.*; 12. 29 f.; Pliny, *N. H.*, 4. 81; cf. Schmidt, *loc. cit.*, 292-
295; Mommsen, *Rom. Prov.*, I, 215 f.
[87] Charlesworth in *C. A. H.*, X, 619.
[88] *Gesch. d. röm. Kaiserz.*, II, i, 30.   [89] Tac., 2. 46. 6.

Tiberius was more proud of his settlements in Germany and Armenia "because he had maintained peace by diplomacy, than if he had won a war by campaigning," [90] it is distinctly to Drusus' credit that his success was diplomatic, not military. Naturally the directing mind was Tiberius' and he properly claimed the glory as his own, but the officer who actually executes his chief's plans and orders is due his own meed of praise. And in the exiguity of our information about Drusus in the years of the Illyrian command, Dessau's final slur is surely gratuitous.[91]

Rome received simultaneously the news that Germanicus had crowned Artaxias king of Armenia and that Drusus had settled affairs in Bohemia by the creation of the client kingdom of Vannius. Ovations were decreed to both governors.[92] It was probably planned that both should celebrate together the ovations decreed together for achievements of the same year; but then Germanicus died in the East and the trial of Piso supervened; Drusus celebrated his ovation alone in 20. Also in commemoration of the two diplomatic victories, triumphal arches were erected, one on either side of the temple of Mars Ultor in the Augustan forum, bearing statues of Germanicus and Drusus respectively.[93] That of Drusus, we have lately learned from the *Fasti* of Ostia, was dedicated 26 February, A. D. 30.[94]

---

[90] Tac., 2. 64. 2.

[91] Drusus' command in Illyricum seems the most probable occasion for the service of T. Raius Crispinus as his staff orderly, *C. I. L.*, IX, 4121.

[92] Tac., 2. 64. 1.

[93] Tac., 2. 64. 2; *C. I. L.*, VI, 31199 (= 911); 31200 (= 912). Cf. Platner-Ashby, *Topogr. Dict.*, 39, 220.

[94] *C. I. L.*, XIV, 4533. Does not the arch of Germanicus and Drusus at Spoletium, *C. I. L.*, XI, 4777, probably commemorate the same events?

Some time in 19, it appears, Drusus and Livilla had returned to Rome, for their twins were born there at the end of that year.[95] Early in 20 Agrippina arrived in Italy bringing home the ashes of Germanicus. The funeral procession on arrival in Tarracina was met by Drusus and his brother Claudius together with Germanicus' children, Nero, Drusus, Agrippina and Drusilla, who had been in Rome; the other two, Gaius and Julia, had been in Syria with their parents. Following the military funeral in Rome, the populace persisted in its mourning until Tiberius found it necessary to issue an edict calling upon the people to return to normal life and business. The imminence of the Megalesian games was some aid toward the restoration of normality.[96]

It must, therefore, have been the end of March A. D. 20 by now, and Drusus set out again for Illyricum.[97] But he cannot have stayed in his province more than three or four weeks, since he was in Rome again for Piso's trial, which must have commenced rather early in May.[98] In the brief interim, however, he had a

---

[95] *Supra*, 96.   [96] Tac., 3. 1-6.   [97] *Id.*, 3. 7. 1.

[98] *Id.*, 3. 11. 1. The following chronological data are clear: on one day the Senatorial court convened and was charged by Tiberius (Tac., 3. 12. 1). The prosecution had two days to present its case and, after an interval of six days, the defense three (Tac., 3. 13. 1). There was a *comperendinatio* (Tac., 3. 15. 4, " redintegratamque accusationem "). The prosecution occupied another day (Tac., 3. 15. 4 f.). The next day Piso was found dead by suicide (Tac., 3. 15. 6). A day (perhaps the same one) seems to have been devoted to Tiberius' questioning of Marcus Piso, the reading of Piso's last protestations of innocence and the exoneration of his son Marcus (Tac., 3. 16. 3-17. 1). The defense of Plancina took another two days (Tac., 3. 17. 6). At least a day must have been consumed in the debate on motions for sentence (Tac., 3. 17. 8-18. 5). An interval of a few days (Tac., 3. 19. 1) followed before Tiberius rewarded the prosecutors with priesthoods. The case had thus taken almost three weeks. Drusus then left the capital to recover his auspices and presently (" mox ") re-entered in ovation—28 May (Tac., 3. 19. 4).

visit in Delmatia from Piso, on his way back from Syria to Rome to stand trial for the murder of Germanicus, and in the event for high treason also. Piso seems to have expected to find Drusus more gratified at becoming next in line to the throne by Germanicus' death than grieved at the loss of his brother. In this he was deluded; Drusus said that if rumors were correct he was first among the bereaved, but that he hoped reports were false and Germanicus' death would bring no one to ruin. Tacitus reports a current belief that Tiberius had instructed Drusus to speak to this effect, "since the otherwise ingenuous and affable young man on this occasion employed the subtleties of an older man." But one does not see in Drusus' declaration any lack of candor.[99]

Piso, failing thus to win any support from Drusus, went on to Rome, shortly followed by his recent host. Drusus, postponing his ovation, entered the capital. And it appears from Tiberius' reference to him in his address at the commencement of the trial, that he was in attendance; also his name was included in the motion of Valerius Messalinus, after the conviction of Piso, " ob vindictam Germanici grates agendas."[100] Some few days after the conclusion of the trial, Drusus left Rome in order to resume his proconsular imperium and on 28 May entered the city in ovation.[101]

[99] Tac., 3. 8.

[100] Id., 3. 9; 3. 11. 1; 3. 12. 11; 3. 18. 4. For a full account of the trial of Piso cf. my Criminal Trials, 36-51.

[101] Tac., 3. 19. 4; C. I. L., XIV, 244 (Fasti Ost.): " V. K. IVN. DRUSUS (Caesar) TRIUMPHAVIT EX ILL (yrico) ." On the seventh anniversary of this event, Gaius Fulvius Chryses, magister pagi Armentini minor (is), made a dedication to the genius of Tiberius, C. I. L., VI, 251 (= 30724 = Dess., 6080).

Just before and after the *Ludi Magni Romani* (4-19 September) in the same year, occurred the trial of Aemilia Lepida for *falsum* and perhaps also for adultery and murder.[102] Indictment for treason also had been sought on the ground that Lepida had consulted astrologers " in domum Caesaris," but that charge was not admitted. Tiberius presided in person at the trial, and Drusus was in attendance as consul-designate. The trial moved toward an inevitable conviction, which would certainly be unpopular with the general public whose favor and sympathy the defendant had courted and won. Tiberius endeavored to save Drusus odium by dispensing him from the obligation of making the first motion for a verdict.[103] Drusus subsequently cast his vote in favor of the legal penalty, although motions to moderate that sentence had been made by some senators.

On 1 January the next year A. D. 21 Drusus entered upon his second consulship. That he had the Emperor as his colleague represented official recognition of his status as Tiberius' now intended successor—Germanicus had been consul with Tiberius in 18, and Sejanus was to be similarly recognized in 31. Tiberius almost immediately withdrew to Campania, and retained the magistracy only three months,[104] nor do we hear of a suffect consul in his place. It is by no means incredible that the gossips of Rome, as Dio relates,[105] considered ominous for Drusus his association with his father in

---

[102] Tac., 3. 22 f. For a full discussion of the case cf. my *Criminal Trials*, 51-56.
[103] I have argued this interpretation of Tacitus' statement, *op. cit.*, 55.
[104] Tac., 3. 31. 1 f.; Suet., 26. 2; cf. *C. I. L.*, II, 5943; VI, 10051 (= Dess., 5283); 32340; X, 1333.
[105] 57. 20. 1 f.

the chief magistracy. For Quintilius Varus and Calpurnius Piso, Tiberius' colleagues in his first two consulships, had both died by suicide, the one in defeat, the other under indictment for high treason, and Germanicus was commonly, even if erroneously, believed to have been murdered by Piso.[106]

According to Tacitus, Tiberius gave out as the reason for his retirement from the capital the need of benefiting his health.[107] Nor need one too readily reject the possibility—Tiberius was sixty-one—in spite of Suetonius' assertion: " valitudine prosperrima usus est, tempore quidem principatus paene toto prope inlaesa."[108] But the historian suggests instead two other motives, that he had begun to consider a prolonged retirement, and that he wished Drusus to have the sole responsibility of the consulship. The magistracy and the year did, at all events, provide Drusus with some considerable experience. We hear of him repeatedly in connection with sessions of the Senate and may with probability assume his presidency of the House on most other occasions, even though our sources do not name him.

He is said to have won favor by mediating a private quarrel which had made its acrimonius way to the floor of the Senate. An ex-praetor, Domitius Corbulo, complained of the affront that Lucius Sulla, a youthful noble, had refused to give up his seat to Corbulo at a gladiatorial show. Interested persons rallied to the side of each, Corbulo's contemporaries and those with a conservative regard for ancestral custom on the one

---

[106] Drusus' subsequent assassination and the execution of Sejanus completed an astonishing series of coincidences.
[107] Tac., 3. 31. 2. [108] Suet., 68. 4.

side, Mamercus Scaurus, Lucius Arruntius and other kinsmen to Sulla's support. Speeches were delivered and precedents rehearsed. Finally Drusus spoke in a manner which calmed the ruffled tempers, and Scaurus on behalf of Sulla, whose uncle and step-father he was, made some sort of satisfaction to Corbulo.[109] The incident seems hardly to have merited discussion in the Senate; and one is a little surprised to encounter Drusus in the rôle of a mediator!

Gaius Cestius in particular, and other senators raised the problem of the right of asylum, and appealed to Drusus to suppress its abuse. Drusus brought to trial Annia Rufilla on a charge of *iniuria*—she had insulted Cestius against whom she bore a grudge, and dared him to take action, claiming the asylum of Tiberius' image. She was convicted and imprisoned; and the case seems to have set a precedent which was still recognized over a century later.[110] Drusus was rightly credited with the checking of the abuse. He also received applause, it is not quite clear why, for the punishment of the calumniators of a praetor, Magius Caecilianus. Considius Aequus and Caelius Cursor had charged him with treason; he was acquitted and they, in turn, were indicted for *calumnia* and punished, " auctore principe ac decreto senatus." Drusus' part in the case can only be guessed; perhaps only presiding over the Senatorial Court, perhaps he was also instrumental in bringing the indictment for *calumnia*.

With another criminal case Drusus' association was much less felicitous. He had been gravely ill, seemingly some time in this year, and Clutorius Priscus, a fatuous

[109] Tac., 3. 31. 3-6.   [110] *Id.*, 3. 36; *Criminal Trials*, 58-60.

poet, in anticipation of his death, had composed and read before an audience a poem in his honor and memory, hoping to repeat the success of a similar effort after Germanicus' death, which had won an honorarium from Tiberius. Upon Drusus' recovery, Priscus was indicted. Unjustly and unfortunately Drusus evidently presided at the trial. Not only was the offense regarded as treason, which legally it was not (for the law of treason did not comprehend the emperor's heir), but the penalty inflicted exceeded even that for treason. On motion of the consul-designate, Haterius Agrippa, Priscus was condemned to death, although Manius Lepidus moved the lesser, but still unreasonable, penalty of banishment and confiscation. It seems indubitable that the motions for sentence were at the instance or with the knowledge of Drusus. There came at once to the Senate an angry demand from Tiberius for a decree providing that judgments of the Senate should not be executed until ten days after filing.[111]

The other business transacted by the Senate during this year of Drusus' second consulship, narrated by our sources without mention of his name, but presumably engaging his attention none the less, may be indicated in summary fashion: Corbulo's prosecution of contractors and municipal magistrates for fraud in highway construction; [112] Tiberius' report of the resumption of hostilities by Tacfarinas in Africa and the appointment *extra sortem* of Quintus Junius Blaesus as proconsul of that province; [113] the indictment for extortion and treason of

[111] *Id.*, 3. 49-51; Dio, 57. 20. 3 f. I have discussed the case at greater length, *Criminal Trials*, 62 f.

[112] Tac., 3. 31. 7; *Criminal Trials*, 57 f.

[113] Tac., 3. 32, 35; cf. *infra*, 138.

Caesius Cordus, the proconsul of Crete;[114] the conviction of Antistius Vetus for high treason;[115] Tiberius' report of the outbreak and suppression of the revolt in Gaul led by Julius Sacrovir and Julius Florus, together with his justification, in reply to criticism, of his failure to go, or send Drusus, to Gaul—it was not seemly for the Emperor or his son to attend in person to a purely local disturbance—and a statement that he planned now to visit Gaul; vows for his safe journey and decrees of thanksgiving and other honors;[116] an adulatory motion of Cornelius Dolabella and the communication of Tiberius rejecting it;[117] and the request by Tiberius of the honor of a public funeral for the late Publius Sulpicius Quirinius.[118]

Finally, under an *egressio relationis*, when the appointment of the African proconsul was being debated, Aulus Caecina Severus moved that magistrates with commands in senatorial provinces be forbidden to have their wives accompany them. The discussion included those remarks of Drusus which have been earlier mentioned[119] as the sole and very tenuous evidence that his marriage with Livilla was a happy one, but the motion did not come to vote.[120]

As his second consulship, with the Emperor for his colleague, had indicated Drusus' designation as heir, so in the next year, A. D. 22, that position was reaffirmed with the conferring of the tribunician power. Tiberius wrote from Campania to the Senate asking the

---

[114] Tac., 3. 38. 1; *Criminal Trials*, 61.
[115] Tac., 3. 38. 2 f.; *Criminal Trials*, 62.
[116] Tac., 3. 47. 1-3.
[117] *Id.*, 3. 47. 4 f.   [119] *Supra*, 98.
[118] *Id.*, 3. 48. 1.   [120] Tac., 3. 33 f.

association of Drusus with himself in that authority. The Senate need not have been consulted, for the Emperor had the right to confer the power upon a colleague;[121] but it was Tiberius' habit to defer to the Senate, to seek its cooperation with him in the duties of administration.[122] In his message the Emperor invoked the gods' blessing on his plans for the State and modestly recited Drusus' qualifications: he was married and had three children (Julia and the twins), and was now of the age at which Tiberius had been associated by Augustus in the tribunician power; he had had eight years of administrative experience, including the suppression of the Pannonian mutiny and the governorship of Illyricum, had received a triumph (ovation) and had twice held the consulship; he was therefore familiar with the functions he was being called upon to fulfill.[123]

The Senate took the occasion to add motions of adulation—statues of Tiberius and Drusus, altars, temples and triumphal arches. Marcus Junius Silanus proposed that the tribunician power be employed, instead of the names of the consuls, as the official method of dating;[124] and Quintus Haterius that the decrees of

[121] Mommsen, Staatsr., II[3], 1161. [122] Cf. supra, 78 ff. [123] Tac., 3. 56.
[124] Silanus is usually identified as the consul of A. D. 15 (so Nipperdey and Furneaux, ad Tac., 3. 57. 2, and Dessau, Prosop., I, 551). He was the father-in-law of Gaius, and is said by Dio, 59. 8. 5, to have been held in such honor by Tiberius that the Emperor would hear no appeal from his judicial decisions. In dependence on his potentia, his brother Decimus in A. D. 20 petitioned return from banishment. It seems unlikely that a person of such standing felt any need to resort to such flattery as this, or that a person given to such flattery would have won the esteem of Tiberius as Silanus had. Dessau, loc. cit., has some doubt of the identification: " nisi hic intellegitur is qui sequitur," viz. the consul of A. D. 19, proconsul of Africa under Tiberius and Gaius. It is perhaps better to ascribe the present motion to him.

that session be engraved on a gold tablet in the *curia*.[125] Tiberius apparently voided all the proposals, although Tacitus says only " caerimonias temperavit," but selected that of Haterius for specific censure as " contra patrium morem." [126]

Drusus, who was in Campania, presumably with Tiberius, wrote to acknowledge his investiture with the power. His letter was, says Tacitus, deferentially phrased, but provoked criticism as a manifestation of arrogance; for there was a strong feeling in Rome that Drusus should have presented himself at the capital and to the Senate.[127] The precise date of the commencement of Drusus' *tribunicia potestas* is not known; but it is possible to set it confidently within the first four or five months of A. D. 22, with much probability in March or April.[128] Our sources make no reference to any exercise of the power.

Some time in the next year, A. D. 23, Drusus again fell ill; the ailment lingered; and finally Drusus died, 14 September, " morbo et intemperantia " Tiberius believed.[129] But because Tiberius, following his usual habit,[130] had refused to let even his son's grave illness interfere with his devotion to the business of the State and had regularly attended the meetings of the Senate, there were those who bitterly criticized his conduct and

[125] Tac., 3. 57.
[126] *Id.*, 3. 59. 2; cf. *supra*, 71.
[127] Tac., 3. 59. 3-6.
[128] *A. J. P.*, 61 (1940), 457-459. The principal evidence is Tac., 3. 56. 1; 3. 59. 2 f.; 3. 64. 1 f., combined with *Fasti Praenestini* (*C. I. L.*, I², p. 236) for 23 April.
[129] Suet., 62. 1; 39; Tac., 4. 8, 10, 11; Dio, 57. 22. 3 ff.; and for the date *Fasti Oppii Maiores, C. I. L.*, VI, 32493; cf. Leuze in *Jahresber. Altertumswiss.*, 227 (1930, III) 102, 139; cf. *C. I. L.*, X, 6638 (= I², p. 248).
[130] Cf. *supra*, 72.

believed him guilty of causing his son's death, a version which Tacitus [131] and Dio [131] record, but take pains to refute and reject. Only eight years later did the real cause of death become known.[132]

The Emperor came before the Senate, and, finding the consuls seated upon the lower benches in token of mourning, bade them take their usual places. With good self-control he addressed the House. He was well aware that his appearance there would subject him to criticism; most persons in similar bereavement could not endure private intercourse with closest intimates. But he found his consolation in the embrace of the State.[133] Then, according to Tacitus, " memoriae Drusi eadem quae in Germanicum decernuntur, plerisque additis." [134] From this statement it appears that Drusus' name was inserted in the Salic hymn; a curule chair crowned with an oak-wreath executed in precious materials was set with those of the Sodales Augustales in the theatre on festal occasions; his statue in ivory was added to the procession at the circensian games; it was decreed that only a member of the Julian family might succeed him as flamen and as augur; [135] the equestrian order named a block of its seats in the theatre after him and carried his statue in their annual review.[136] The fragmentary inscription which records the posthumous honors of Drusus, beside possible references to some of those just catalogued from Tacitus, mentions that a silver *clupeus* which the knights had dedicated to Drusus was to lead their review-parade.[137] And the thirty five tribes of the

---

[131] *Loc. cit.*
[132] Cf. *infra*, 143-145.
[133] Tac., 4. 8; Dio, 57. 22. 4a.
[134] Tac., 4. 9. 2.
[135] We know that his nephew Nero was flamen, e. g., *C. I. L.*, VI, 887 (= Dess., 183); 913 (= Dess., 182); III, 2808 (= Dess., 7156).
[136] Cf. Tac., 2. 83.
[137] *C. I. L.*, VI, 31200; cf. 31199.

plebs urbana dedicated an inscription and statue, " aere conlato." [138]

Drusus' body lay in state upon the rostra, and Nero, his nephew and son-in-law, delivered a funeral eulogy. On the analogy afforded in the funeral of Augustus with eulogies by Drusus and Tiberius, we may assume that Nero's was of personal and private character. Tiberius then pronounced an eulogy over his son, which we may similarly suppose was for the State.[139] We have from Seneca, who may conceivably have been present, a vivid description of the scene. " Stetit in conspectu posito corpore, interiecto tantummodo velamento, quod pontificis oculos a funere arceret, et flente populo Romano non flexit vultum; experiendum se dedit Seiano ad latus stanti, quam patienter posset suos perdere." [140] Tacitus alleges that the mourning of the people was insincere, that secretly they rejoiced at the consequent revival of the prospects of Germanicus' house.[141] But Seneca has no hint that the grief was not genuine; and we shall see that, if Drusus was not fanatically idolized as Germanicus had been, he did have none the less his own popularity; [142] and there was a group politically adherent to him as there was also a party of Germanicus and his family.[143] The funeral procession was noteworthy for the appearance of statues of Aeneas, the Alban kings, Romulus, the Sabine nobility, Attus Clausus, and a long line of Claudii.[144]

The funeral was scarcely past when Tiberius returned

---

[138] Dess., 168 (= *C. I. L.*, VI, 910).

[139] Dio, 57. 22. 4a; Tac., 4. 12. 1; cf. *supra*, 106 and references there.

[140] Sen., *ad Marc.*, 15. 3.

[141] Tac., *loc. cit.*

[142] Cf. *infra*, 152 f.

[143] Cf. *supra*, 112 f., 52.

[144] Tac., 4. 9. 3. Cf. *supra*, 112.

with complete application to his duties of State, the courts and the Senate, forbidding that there should be any protracted *iustitium*.[145] But we hear that Agrippa I departed Rome because Tiberius could not bear the sight of those who had been close friends of Drusus.[146] When rather tardily, however, an embassy came from Ilium bearing condolences to the Emperor for his son's loss, he mockingly expressed his regrets for their loss of a distinguished fellow-citizen, Hector.[147]

Certain other facts of Drusus' public life are not datable and may be set down here. Several towns honored themselves and him by electing Drusus to local magistracies. He was dictator (according to Dessau) at Aricia,[148] *duovir quinquennalis* at Aquinum, Volaterrae, Praeneste (together with Germanicus), and at some other unidentifiable town, and hipparch at Cyzicus.[149] He was *duovir* of the *Colonia Julia Gemella Acci* and *quattuorvir* at Carteia, with Germanicus as his colleague in both cases.[150] I believe he was *quattuorvir quinquennalis* at Salonae. An inscription found there reads: " L. Anicio L.f. | Paetinati | IIII vir. iure dic. | quinquennal. prae. | quinq. Drusi Caesar. | Germanici praefec. | quinq. P. Dolabellae | pontifici flamini Iuliae Augustae praef. | fabr. | praefectur. Phariac. | Salonitan." [151] Mommsen comments: " Germanicus Drusi senioris filius, adoptatus a Tiberio, qui sine dubio intel-

---

[145] Tac., 4.13.1; Suet., 52.1.

[146] Jos., *Ant.*, 18.146.

[147] Suet., 52.2; cf. Scott, *A.J.P.*, 53 (1932), 146 f.

[148] *E.E.*, VII, 1236.

[149] *C.I.L.*, X, 5393, 5394; XI, 7066; XIV, 2964 ii 5; VI, 29715; *I.G.R.*, IV, 187.

[150] Heiss, *Monnaies antiques de l'Espagne*, 257, 332.

[151] *C.I.L.*, III, 14712 (= Dess., 7160).

legitur, nusquam praeterea quod sciam Drusi nomine utitur, errore ut videtur ei tributo ab homine provinciali." Dessau annotates: " Est Drusus Germanici filius, Germanicus dictus etiam " in the Ticinum inscription of the imperial family (cf. *supra* 102 and note 1) on which he remarks; "mirum hunc Drusum . . . hic pro Caesare dici Germanicum." But, most strangely, both editors ignore that our Drusus by reason of his governorship of Illyricum is much the most likely member of the imperial family to be thus honored at Salonae. Nothing is more natural and probable than that Salonae which had elected Dolabella, the governor of Delmatia, *quattuorvir*, should then similarly elect Drusus Caesar, when he came to govern Delmatia and neighboring territories with *maius imperium*. And since Dolabella was in Delmatia at least as early as 14, and Drusus was in Illyricum until 20, there was time for a second election of *quattuorviri quinquennales* (Dolabella in 14 or 15, and Drusus in 19 or 20). And finally, while our Drusus did not bear the name Germanicus, it is given to him (as also to Tiberius!) in a Greek inscription.[152]

Drusus makes a solitary appearance with respect to public works. Together with his father he gave a city gate to Laus Pompeia.[153]

The *Liber Coloniarum* ascribes to Drusus colonies at Anagnia, Calagna and Cereatae Mariana (*sic*).[154] But Anagnia was still a *municipium*, and Calagna is an error of dittography for Anagnia; " Cereatini, qui Mariani cognominantur " are listed by Pliny among *oppida*.[155]

[152] *I. G.*, VII, 3103.   [153] *C. I. L.*, V, 6358.
[154] *Lib. Colon.*, pp. 230 line 17, 231 line 17, 233 line 8; this evidence is accepted for Anagnia and Cereatae by Ciaceri, *Tiberio, Successore di Augusto*, 218.
[155] P. W., I, 2025, III, 1327; Pliny, N. H., 3. 63.

III. DRUSUS AND SEJANUS

When Drusus set out for Pannonia to deal with the mutiny there in August-September of A. D. 14, one of the members of his staff was Lucius Aelius Sejanus, then colleague of his father Lucius Seius Strabo in the prefecture of the praetorian guard. Tiberius appointed him to be "rector" to Drusus on the Pannonian mission.[1] Subsequently the progressive rise of Sejanus toward power roused Drusus' opposition and jealousy. Their relations were punctuated by a quarrel which ended in fisticuffs on both sides. And finally Drusus fell the first victim when Sejanus conspired to win for himself Tiberius' throne.

We must, therefore, attempt to trace the course of Sejanus' advancing career (which is difficult because chronological data are few), marking those points especially where Sejanus and Drusus came into contact and conflict; and endeavor to date the commencement of the plot against Drusus' life. That will be also the date, approximately, of Sejanus' conception of the ambition to rule the Empire,[2] which, I believe, no one previously has tried to place in time.

After his appointment to the staff of Drusus in Pannonia, the next dated reference to Sejanus is the statement of Dio,[3] that after the death of Germanicus, that is in 20 or at the end of 19, Tiberius bestowed *ornamenta praetoria* upon him and made him his advisor

---

[1] *Supra*, 108. [2] Cf. Dio, 57. 22. 2.

[3] 57. 19. 7 (Xiphilinus). In the meantime Sejanus had become sole praetorian prefect when his father was appointed to Egypt, Dio, 57. 19. 6.

and adjutant. Also in 20 Sejanus' daughter was betrothed to Drusus, the son of Claudius, who, however, died a few days later. And in that connection Tacitus reports that Sejanus was now suspected of having lofty ambitions and that Tiberius was censured for excessively (or gratuitously) exalting him.[4] The same year he was associated with the trial of Piso, according to an oral tradition preserved by Tacitus.[5] It was alleged that Piso was tricked by the empty promises of Sejanus into withholding from the court the evidence afforded by his *mandata* from the Emperor. Whatever interpretation one places upon the incident, if it be accepted as historical at all, Sejanus appears as Tiberius' adjutant.[6]

In A. D. 21 Blaesus, Sejanus' uncle, received appointment as proconsul of Africa to conduct the war against Tacfarinas; and Tacitus says that his relation to Sejanus was a cogent, though unmentioned, reason for his selection instead of Lepidus, Tiberius' other nominee.[7] It is true that Blaesus was qualified for the command and Lepidus was not; but that circumstance hardly precludes either the possibility that Tiberius nominated Blaesus rather than some other competent general out of favor to Sejanus, or the possibility that the senators were moved somewhat in their decision by the prestige of Sejanus. And the next year, when Blaesus was granted *ornamenta triumphalia* for his military successes in Africa, Tiberius stated explicitly that honor to Sejanus motivated the award to his uncle.[8]

The year 22 provides two other mentions of Sejanus.

---

[4] Tac. 3. 29. 5 f.; M has *ultra*; Nipp. writes *ultro*. Cf. Suet., *Claud.*, 27. 1.
[5] Tac., 3. 16. 1.   [7] Tac., 3. 35. 2.
[6] Cf. *Criminal Trials*, 51, n. 160.   [8] *Id.*, 3. 72. 6.

Junius Otho, praetor in that year, is said by Tacitus to have become a senator by the influence of Sejanus.[9] And when fire destroyed the theatre of Pompey, Sejanus was on the scene and was credited with the success of preventing the fire's spread to other buildings; the Senate therefore voted a statue of him in the theatre.[10]

So many chronological data we have for the career of Sejanus in the early years of Tiberius' reign. It is possible to expand this outline a little from the brief summaries (without dates) of Tacitus and Velleius.

It has been mentioned that when Tiberius conferred *ornamenta praetoria*, according to Dio (Xiphilinus), he made Sejanus σύμβουλον καὶ ὑπηρέτην πρὸς πάντα.[11] It cannot be mere coincidence that Velleius writes: " singularem principalium onerum *adiutorem in omnia* habuit atque habet ": [12] and Tacitus: "facili Tiberio atque ita prono, ut *socium laborum* non modo in sermonibus, sed apud patres et populum celebraret "; [13] and that Tacitus again records that Drusus complained "incolumi filio *adiutorem imperii* alium vocari." [14] The four phrases obviously allude to the same incident, which appears to have been a statement by Tiberius before the Senate, naming Sejanus officially or semi-officially as his adjutant. And, if Dio may be thus far trusted, the date was A. D. 20 or the last months of 19—it is placed between the death of Germanicus and Drusus' consulship, 10 October, 19—1 January 21.

Tacitus presents a thumb-nail sketch of Sejanus'

[9] *Id.*, 3. 66. 4.
[10] *Id.*, 3. 72. 4 f.; cf. Sen., *ad Marc.*, 22. 4; Dio, 57. 21. 3 dates it in the next year.
[11] Dio, 57. 19. 7.
[12] Vell., 2. 127. 3.
[13] Tac., 4. 2. 4; cf. Dio, 58, 4. 3.
[14] Tac., 4. 7. 2.

career, obviously arranged in chronological order, which may here be quoted in full, but divided into the successive stages of the prefect's advance and with dates assigned where possible. After characterizing Sejanus, Tacitus writes:

(1) "Vim praefecturae [A. D. 14, Tac., 1. 24. 3] modicam antea intendit,

(2) dispersas per urbem cohortes una in castra conducendo, ut simul imperia acciperent numeroque et robore et visu inter se fiducia ipsis, in ceteros metus oreretur. Praetendebat lascivire militem diductum; si quid subitum ingruat, maiore auxilio pariter subveniri; et severius acturos, si vallum statuatur procul urbis inlecebris.

(3) Ut perfecta sunt castra,

(4) inrepere paulatim militares animos adeundo, appellando; simul centuriones ac tribunos ipse deligere.

(5) Neque senatorio ambitu abstinebat clientes suos honoribus aut provinciis ornandi [Junius Otho, praetor in 22, would have been quaestor presumably in 20 and XXvir before that, so Sejanus' senatorial patronage may be dated, say, A. D. 18/19 circa.],

(6) facili Tiberio atque ita prono, ut socium laborum non modo in sermonibus, sed apud patres et populum celebraret [A. D. 20]

(7) colique per theatra [A. D. 22] et fora effigies eius interque principia legionum sineret." [15]

In a somewhat similar, but shorter, passage Tacitus represents the attitude and speech of Drusus: "Sejanus

[15] Id., 4. 2.

incipiente adhuc potentia bonis consiliis notescere volebat, et ultor [*sc.* Drusus] metuebatur non occultus odii, set crebro querens incolumi filio adiutorem imperii alium vocari. Et quantum superesse, ut collega dicatur? Primas dominandi spes in arduo: ubi sis ingressus, adesse studia et ministros. Exstructa iam sponte praefecti castra, datos in manum milites; cerni effigiem eius in monimentis Cn. Pompei; communes illi cum familia Drusorum fore nepotes [as Nipperdey noted, there were only a few days during which this statement would have been accurate, and that prior to the placing of Sejanus' statue in the theatre]: precandam post haec modestiam, ut contentus esset." [16]

Velleius, having characterized Sejanus and recounted from Roman history numerous examples of the ennoblement of more or less humble persons by meritorious service to the State, writes: [17] " Haec naturalis exempli imitatio ad experiendum Seianum Caesarem, ad iuvanda vero onera principis Seianum propulit [A. D. 20] [18] senatumque et populum Romanum eo perduxit, ut, quod usu optimum intellegit, id in tutelam securitatis suae libenter advocet " [*circa* A. D. 24, if the interpretation offered *supra* 30, is found acceptable].

At some date in these years 14 to 22 Drusus and Sejanus quarreled violently and exchanged blows. Three passages in our sources mention this fight, Tacitus' account under A. D. 23 of the events which culminated in the assasination of Drusus, and Dio's records of the years 15 and 23. [19] Scott has discussed these,

---

[16] *Id.*, 4. 7. 2-4. [17] Vell., 2. 128. 4.
[18] Cf. Vell., 2. 127. 3 quoted *supra*, 139.
[19] Tac., 4. 3. 2; Dio, 57. 14. 9; 57. 22. 1. The former passage of Dio identifies Sejanus not by name but only as a distinguished knight.

proving conclusively that they refer to the same incident and that the incident cannot be dated in 23; he
therefore assigns it to 15, the other year under which
Dio mentions it.²⁰ But that passage of Dio, while it does
not contain a warning ποτέ as does the one relating to
23, is a general characterization of Drusus, motivated
by mention of his conduct in the consulship and illustrated by two anecdotes of which the fight with Sejanus
is one. Neither anecdote can be assigned with any
assurance to 15. And, further, such a dating seems
prima facie much too early for the antipathy and
antagonism of Drusus toward a rival, which produced
the openly violent quarrel, as Tacitus states. That
rivalry points rather to A. D. 20 when Sejanus became
Tiberius' *socius laborum* and Drusus complained " adiutorem imperii alium vocari." Nothing in Sejanus' career
before that year, so far as we know it, seems to present
him clearly in the light of a probable rival to Drusus.
That incident does. Dio cites as the provocation that
Sejanus was ἐπί τε τῇ ἰσχύι καὶ ἐπὶ τῷ ἀξιώματι ὑπερ
μαζήσας τά τε ἄλλα ὑπέρογχος. That, too, accords well
with his promotion and preferment in A. D. 20. It would
not be a very serious objection, I think, that Dio calls
Sejanus " distinguished knight " in the account of the
fist-fight (and that is necessary to Scott's convincing
interpretation of Drusus' nickname of " Castor "), while
the *ornamenta praetoria* represented elevation to senatorial rank.²¹ The encounter between Drusus and Se-

²⁰ *C. P.*, 25 (1930), 155 ff.
²¹ Five years later, when Sejanus sought marriage with Livilla, both he
and Tiberius could think and write of him as a knight apparently, Tac.,
4. 39, 40.

janus can be placed, not without some confidence, in A. D. 20.

"Recens ira" because of the blows suffered at Drusus' hands was, according to Tacitus,[22] the motivation for Sejanus' plot against Drusus' life. And that plot was the first step taken to advance Sejanus' ambition for the imperial position. That high ambition was newly conceived. For Tacitus writes, immediately following the sketch of Sejanus' career from the prefecture of the guard to establishment of his cult (quoted above, 140): "Ceterum plena Caesarum domus, iuvenis filius, nepotes adulti moram cupitis adferebant; et quia vi tot simul corripere intutum, dolus intervalla scelerum poscebat. Placuit tamen occultior via et a Druso incipere, in quem recenti ira ferebatur", then follows Tacitus' account of the fight. To be noted is the singular *iuvenis filius*; not two sons, Germanicus and Drusus, stood in Sejanus' path, but one, Drusus. Again the evidence points to A. D. 20; that was the year when Sejanus, suspected now, according to Tacitus, of lofty aspirations, betrothed his daughter to Claudius' son.[23]

Considering different means of attaining his end, Sejanus decided to attack Drusus through his wife, Livilla. He seduced her into adulterous relations, and promising her marriage with him and a share of the imperial power, urged her to the murder of her husband. The two conspirators took into their confidence Eudemus, the intimate friend and the personal physician (according to Pliny [24] also the paramour) of Livilla. Sejanus then divorced his wife, Apicata, so that Livilla

[22] 4. 3. 1; cf. Dio, 57. 22. 1 f.   [23] Cf. *supra*, 138.   [24] *N. H.*, 29. 20.

should not be suspicious of his devotion to herself. " Sed magnitudo facinoris metum prolationes, diversa interdum consilia adferebat," remarks Tacitus.[25]

Thus it was not until more than two years later, in A. D. 23, that the conspiracy came to fruition. Of the interim, naturally, we know little that bears on the plot. Sejanus, writes Tacitus, " incipiente adhuc potentia bonis consiliis notescere volebat." [26] His uncle Blaesus won advancement and honor because of his relation to Sejanus. And the prefect's activity on the occasion of the fire in Pompey's theatre brought himself the honor of a statue there. Meantime Drusus returned to Rome from Illyricum, celebrated his ovation in 20, and held the consulship the next year. In 21 also he underwent the severe illness which brought ill fate to Clutorius Priscus. Was that illness possibly an abortive attempt by Sejanus to poison Drusus? And in 22 he was vested with the tribunician power. His hatred of Sejanus served as a check upon the prefect, according to Tacitus. And he complained frequently in public and in private that while the Emperor's son lived, another was named *adiutor imperii*; how far short was that of his being named colleague? at its beginning the path to power is steep; when you have begun to climb, zealous supporters appear to aid; the prefect already had a camp built at his behest and control of troops; now his likeness was to be seen in the theatre which was Pompey's

---

[25] 4. 3. 6. It has been doubted that Drusus died by other than natural causes; it has also been doubted that, if he was murdered, Livilla had any complicity in the guilt. I am myself convinced both of the murder and of Livilla's guilt; I have argued the questions elsewhere and need here say only that my opinion remains the same; cf. my *Criminal Trials*, 119 ff. and references there.

[26] 4. 7. 2.

monument; he was to be grandfather to the grandsons of the Drusi; after all this, might the gods grant him the moderation to be satisfied.

Livilla betrayed to Sejanus what was said by Drusus in private. The prefect decided action was necessary and slow poison was administered through the agency of Lygdus, presumably Drusus' *praegustator*.[27] On 14 September, A. D. 23 Drusus died.[28]

The secret of the plot had been well kept. For eight years it remained unsuspected. In October of 31 Sejanus was denounced for treason, and executed on the 18th of that month. On the 26th his wife Apicata committed suicide after dispatching a letter to Tiberius in which she revealed the facts of his son's death.[29] Apicata, too, had known and kept the secret. It seems that her divorce by Sejanus had been with her consent, that she loved him and wished him success, and that, after his final failure and execution, she avenged him with this deliberate and terrible blow at Tiberius. An alternative explanation of her eight years' silence would be fear of Sejanus while he lived. But that would fail completely to account for her suicide. Rather her suicide testifies to her utter loyalty, throughout and to the end, to her husband and his ambitions.

---

[27] Tac., 4. 7 f.
[28] *Supra*, 132 and references there.
[29] For details cf. my *Criminal Trials*, 110-122.

IV. DRUSUS' APPEARANCE AND CHARACTER

Those members of the Julio-Claudian family who came actually to rule are described for us by Suetonius, but we have no such word-picture of Drusus. We are, therefore, limited to the evidence of sculpture and the coins for our knowledge of how Drusus looked. *Asses* from the Roman mint in A. D. 23/24 and drachms a decade later issuing from Caesarea-Cappadocia carry Drusus' head as their type,[1] and there is an excellent portrait head at Avignon.[2]

The Avignon head is a partly idealized, partly individual, portrait. It depicts a sensitive, intelligent young man with a distant, dreamy gaze but a determined expression. The hair is stylized in the usual Roman fashion of the period. A few locks fall down upon the middle of the forehead. At the side the hair waves in an S-curve back from the temple to the ear; from the base of the skull it returns again toward the ear, to produce a pleasing pattern. The medium forehead recedes from a pronounced ridge above the bridge of the nose until it is lost underneath the hair. The eyes are set at a moderate depth and heavily shadowed at the corners; their expression is distant, dreamy. The aquiline nose is not very thick, and is well-proportioned to the other features. The cheeks are full and youthful, modelled

---

[1] *B. M. C.*, Tib., 99-101, 171-173, plates 24. 8 and 23. 13; cf. Imhoof-Blumer, *Porträtköpfe auf röm. Münzen*, plate 1. 12. Mattingly dates the *asses* 22/23, but Drusus was not *trib. pot.* II until 23, cf. *supra*, 132.

[2] Espérandieu, *Bas-reliefs de la Gaule*, III, 377, # 2551; cf. Curtius in *Röm. Mitt.*, 49 (1934), 124 f., fig. 4, and plates 6 and 7. For other portraits cf. Bernouilli, *Röm. Ikonogr.*, II, i, 198, 200 f., and plates 9 and 33.

in broad planes relieved only by the prominent lines on either side of nose and mouth. From under the nose the profile recedes to a small pointed chin. The mouth, nicely set in relation to nose and chin, is small and thin, feminine and delicate.

Eyes, mouth and chin are individual; so too, are the general outline of the face, and a few lines and exaggerations which give expression to the countenance. The rest is stylized and idealized. It is a very sensitive and intelligent face, with a good deal of determination in the set expression of the mouth and nose, and the firm, if small, chin. Nor is it difficult to see in the thin, delicate mouth something of that cruelty which so often characterized his action.

Drusus was assiduous and hard-working, an able and very competent man. Dio comments upon his first consulship in 15, that he performed its functions with conscientiousness equal to that of his colleague; [3] and mention of his activity both in that year and as consul II in 21 is quite frequent enough in the sources to substantiate Dio's general statement. In his two major assignments, the suppression of the mutiny in Pannonia and the governorship of Illyricum, he manifested his ability. Attention has already been directed to the striking contrast between Drusus' actions in Pannonia and Germanicus' in Germany. Drusus went without specific instructions, to deal as he thought wise with the situation as he found it. He accepted the responsibility, dealt firmly and forthrightly with the unruly troops, and visited swift and severe punishment upon the individuals guilty of instigating the mutiny. He acted by

[3] Dio, 57. 14. 9.

his own authority, employing the officers of the legions and of the guard to aid him in putting down the mutiny and restoring discipline; the grievances of the troops were to be duly considered by the proper authority in Rome after order and discipline were restored. By contrast, Germanicus had evaded responsibility, forged a communication from Tiberius and, worst of all, tried to conciliate the rank and file by yielding their officers to mob trial and lynch execution by the troops. The competence with which Drusus administered his command in Illyricum and met problems posed by the situation in neighboring Germany is abundantly evidenced by the relative permanence of the arrangements he made. And the performance of his functions as magistrate in Rome seems to have been creditable, so long as his own personal interests and predilections were not involved; but, emphatically, that exception must be made.

If there was not, as we shall see, nobility of character in Drusus, there seems to have been a nobility of manner or bearing or appearance. Ovid's line [4]

nec vigor est Drusi nobilitate minor

may probably be discounted as mere purposeful adulation. But Tacitus, describing Drusus' address to the mutineers, writes, " quamquam rudis dicendi, nobilitate ingenita incusat priora, probat praesentia." [5] And the

---

[4] *Pont.*, 2. 2. 74.

[5] Tac., 1. 29. 1. Gerber and Greef place this occurrence of *nobilitas* under the heading of *de animo*; Nipperdey *ad loc.*, annotates: " in geistigem Sinne "; Furneaux: " This word has here something of a moral sense like that of γεννaιότης, ' generosity.' " Such a sense seems to me inept of Drusus. And Tacitus does not have for Drusus the fervent admiration that he shows for Germanicus—which would afford explana-

resemblance to his father, which seems to be attested,[6] suggests it, for Tiberius assuredly was noble of aspect and bearing.[7]

But, whereas Tiberius was characterized by *moderatio* and *civilitas*, Drusus was arrogant. There is the anecdote of Dio,[8] that Tiberius rebuked Drusus publicly, on some occasion which we cannot identify, " ζῶντος μέν μου οὐδὲν οὔτε βίαιον οὔθ' ὑβριστικὸν πράξεις· ἂν δέ τι καὶ τολμήσῃς, οὐδὲ τελευτήσαντος." There is the evidence of Drusus' claim to eminence of status as a member of the imperial family (notably in the incident of Haterius Agrippa's election to the praetorship and in the indictment of Clutorius Priscus).[9] And while his letter accepting the grant of the tribunician power was, according to Tacitus, deferentially phrased, he was criticized in the Senate on that occasion for arrogance shown in his failure to come to Rome for the investiture. There seems to be some basis in reason for the senatorial attitude; at least, one feels pretty sure that, under identical circumstances, Tiberius (*modestus* and *civilis*) would not have given the same offense. With the arrogance went a hot temper.[10]

These characteristics will, I believe, go far toward explaining Drusus' relations with other members of his family. They were antipathetic to the modesty and self-control of Tiberius. If Drusus and Germanicus were always " egregie concordes," as Tacitus [11] asserts, it may

tion. I should prefer to understand it as referring to Drusus' presence on this occasion, and I notice that John Jackson translates it (Loeb) " dignity."

[6] Cf. *infra*, p. 152.
[7] Suet., 68. 1-3.
[8] 57. 13. 2.

[9] *Supra*, pp. 118 and 129.
[10] Dio, 57. 14. 9; Tac., 4. 3. 2.
[11] 2. 43. 7.

have been because Germanicus shared Drusus' sentiments on their exalted status;[12] and because Germanicus, certainly a far less forceful personality, allowed Drusus the sense of domination in their intercourse (which after all must have been rather limited by reason of their diverse duties and travels). They certainly explain Agrippina's hostility—if it is necessary to explain her dislike of anyone; for she was just as arrogant, domineering and hot-tempered as he. If Drusus was a good father to his nephews after Germanicus' death, we may see the inheritance in some degree from Tiberius of a sense of duty and obligation. The violent anger and bitter intolerance evidenced in his relation with Sejanus are perhaps, given the circumstances and the provocation, venial; but they brought a terrible retribution. Nor were they limited to that relationship; the case of Clutorius Priscus seems to show a vindictive spirit; and Tiberius appears to have feared something of the same kind when he exempted Drusus from making the first motion of sentence in the case of Aemilia Lepida. Nor is the arrogant nature by any means necessarily inconsistent with the fact that Drusus consorted with the disreputable actors' profession.

All this makes one rather suspicious of the statement in Tacitus that he was, ordinarily, " incallidus . . . et facilis iuventa." [13] Candid, yes—but not affable. The remark occurs in the account of Drusus' interview with Gnaeus Piso in Delmatia; Drusus was supposed to have spoken and acted under prompting from Tiberius. It suited the anti-Tiberian tradition to make Drusus affable, except when Tiberius instructed him to be

---

[12] Suggested *supra*, p. 118.   [13] 3. 8. 4.

otherwise. Actually one finds no affability evident in his conduct.

Tacitus twice mentions Drusus' love of luxury. As Tiberius' motive in sending his son to Illyricum is assigned "iuvenem urbano luxu lascivientem melius in castris haberi." [14] Again describing the public esteem of Drusus, the historian writes, " neque luxus in iuvene adeo displicebat "; and adds an allusion to a passion for extravagant building.[15] And epicurean taste is hinted in the amusing trifle, preserved by the elder Pliny,[16] that Drusus, in agreement with Apicius, did not like the young shoots of cabbage.

Worse, he was cruel and bloodthirsty. Dio says [17] that the sharpest swords were called " Drusian " after him. Tacitus says of his punishment of the mutinous soldiers, " promptum ad asperiora ingenium Druso erat." [18] His gratification at the bloodshed of the gladiatorial games is said to have been evident.[19] Voting on an issue which presented a choice between the milder and the more severe, Drusus seems always to have favored the latter; so in punishing citizens for the practise of astrology; so in the case of Aemilia Lepida; so, in the case of Considius Aequus and Caelius Cursor (though it is perhaps not quite just to include that) ; so again in the case of Annia Rufilla, and so, most notably, even if indirectly, in the outrageous execution of Clutorius Priscus.[20]

[14] Tac., 2. 44. 1.

[15] Tac., 3. 37. 3. Since this is not elsewhere recorded of Drusus (but is that necessarily ground for denying its truth?) some editors have emended *aedificationibus* to *ludicris factionibus, ludificationibus, laetificationibus, agitationibus, equitationibus* or *editionibus*.

[16] *N. H.*, 19. 137.   [18] 1. 29. 4.

[17] 57. 13. 1.   [19] Tac., 1. 76. 5.

[20] Cf. *supra*, pp. 116, 126, 128, and 129.

Our sources are united in recording that Drusus had a fondness for alcohol. Dio puts it most strongly: τῇ τε μέθῃ κατακορής, and tells an anecdote in illustration. One night Drusus and some of the praetorian guard were giving assistance at the scene of a fire; when there was a call for water, Drusus ordered, "Pour it out hot!"[21] Tacitus likewise implies that he spent his nights "conviviis."[22] And from Suetonius we learn that Tiberius thought it was "morbo et intemperantia" that his son died.[23] This failing, it may be noted, was perhaps inherited from Tiberius. Pliny writes: "Tiberio principe in senecta iam severo atque etiam saevo; alias et ipsi iuventa ad merum pronior fuerat. . . . Nec alio magis Drusus Caesar regenerasse patrem Tiberium ferebatur."[24]

His life and conduct were dissolute and licentious. Suetonius' phrase is "fluxioris remissiorisque vitae." Dio applies the word ἀσελγέστατος; the "lascivientem" of Tacitus has been quoted above.[25] Finally, Tacitus has a strong hint of sodomy in his mention of Drusus' eunuch Lygdus.[26]

Yet Drusus was popular. This is pretty clearly implied in a passage of Tacitus: "Utrumque [the punishment of Annia Rufilla and the conviction of Considius and Caelius, A. D. 21] in laudem Drusi trahebatur: ab eo in urbe, inter coetus et sermones hominum obversante, secreta patris mitigari. Neque luxus in iuvene

---

[21] Dio, 57. 14. 10.   [23] Suet., *Tib.*, 62. 1; cf. *supra*, 132.
[22] 3. 37. 3.   [24] Pliny, *op. cit.*, 14. 144 f.; cf. Suet., 42. 1.
[25] Suet., 52. 1; Dio, 57. 13. 1; Tac., 2. 44. 1.
[26] Tac., 4. 10. 2. The licentiousness also might be considered to be inherited from Tiberius, if even a part of what the historians record of that Emperor were true.

adeo displicebat: huc potius intenderet, diem aedificationibus, noctem conviviis traheret, quam solus et nullis
voluptatibus avocatus maestam vigilantiam et malas
curas exerceret." [27] And Stuart has shown by a com-
parison of the portrait inscriptions of Germanicus and
Drusus,[28] that the general impression conveyed by
Tacitus of the much greater popularity of Germanicus is
exaggerated and false. He finds evidence of fifty-one
portraits of Germanicus, but ten of these are dated
after Drusus' death in A. D. 23, some occasioned by
Drusus' death, some due to the fact that a son (Gaius)
and a brother (Claudius) later became Emperors. Of
Drusus Stuart finds forty-two portrait inscriptions
(overlooking one more),[29] one of which belongs to the
reign of Claudius. So far, then, as such inscriptions can
provide evidence of the popularity with their contemporaries of Germanicus and Drusus, the two princes
appear very closely on a par.

Clearly Drusus was not an attractive person, popular
though he was with the Roman people. But if one
cannot admire his personality as a private individual,
one must respect him as a public figure—his energy,
his competence, his devotion to duty, his loyalty to
Tiberius, his positive and considerable achievement in
the service of the State. Had he lived to come to power,
the Empire at large would not have fared ill. He was
well-trained by experience *domi militiaeque,* and he had
the capabilities. He would have been, I judge, prototype
of Domitian—absolutist, cruel, domineering and able.

---

[27] Tac., 3. 37. 2 f.
[28] *C. P.,* 35 (1940), 64-67.
[29] *S. E. G.,* I, 387.

ABBREVIATIONS

A. E.	*L'Année Épigraphique.*
A. H. R.	*American Historical Review.*
A. J. P.	*American Journal of Philology.*
B. M. C.	*Catalogue of Coins of the Roman Empire in the British Museum.*
B. M. C.,	
Lydia, etc.	*Catalogue of Greek Coins in the British Museum,* volumes for *Lydia; Troas, Aeolis, Lesbos; Phrygia; Caria.*
C. A. H.	*Cambridge Ancient History.*
C. I. L.	*Corpus Inscriptionum Latinarum.*
Corinth.	*Corinth,* VIII, ii, *Latin Inscriptions.*
C. P.	*Classical Philology.*
Criminal	
Trials	R. S. Rogers, *Criminal Trials and Criminal Legislation under Tiberius.*
Dess.	Dessau, *Inscriptiones Latinae Selectae.*
E. E.	*Ephemeris Epigraphica.*
Forsch. u.	
Fortschr.	*Forschungen und Fortschritte.*
Harv. Theol.	
Rev.	*Harvard Theological Review.*
I. G.	*Inscriptiones Graecae.*
I. G. R. R.	*Inscriptiones Graecae ad Res Romanas pertinentes.*
Inscr. Olymp.	*Die Inschriften von Olympia.*
Jacoby,	
F. G. H.	F. Jacoby, *Fragmente der griechischen Historiker.*
Jahresber.	
Altertumswiss.	*Jahresberichte über die Fortschritte der klassischen Altertumswissenschaft.*
J. R. S.	*Journal of Roman Studies.*
Lib. Colon.	*Liber Coloniarum* in *Accademia dei Lincei, Memorie,* XVI (1920), 55-93, 377-411.
Prosop.	*Prosopographia Imperii Romani,* cited by the initial

155

of the *nomen* and the numerical designation of the individual member of the *gens*; the second edition has been used so far as published, i. e., A. to C.

P. W.   Pauly-Wissowa-Kroll-Mittelhaus, *Real Encyclopädie der classischen Altertumswissenschaft.*

R. E. A.   *Revue des Études Anciennes.*

Rev. Arch.   *Revue Archéologique.*

Rev. Hist.   *Revue Historique.*

Rev. Num.   *Revue Numismatique.*

Rh. M.   *Rheinisches Museum.*

Riv. Stor.
Ant.   *Rivista di Storia Antica.*

Röm. Mitt.   *Mitteilungen des deutschen archaeologischen Instituts, Roemische Abteilung.*

Schanz-
Hosius   Schanz, *Geschichte der römischen Literatur,* 2 Teil, 4th edition revised by C. Hosius.

S. E. G.   *Supplementum Epigraphicum Graecum.*

Sitzb. k. b.
Akad. z.
Münich.   *Sitzungsberichte der königliche bayerische Akademie zu München.*

T. A. P. A.   *Transactions of the American Philological Association.*

SELECT BIBLIOGRAPHY

The following bibliography makes no pretense of being complete. It consists of those items which have been actually cited in the notes, with the addition of a few titles on the general subject of " imperial virtues," included because that field is rather new and not as yet, perhaps, generally familiar.

Alföldi, A., " Insignien und Tracht der römischen Kaiser," in Röm. Mitt., L (1935), 1-171.

Allen, W., " The Political Atmosphere of the Reign of Tiberius," in *T. A. P. A.*, LXXII (1941), 1-25.

Baker, G. P., *Tiberius Caesar*, London, 1929.

Balsdon, J. P. V. D., *The Emperor Gaius (Caligula)*, Oxford, 1934.

———, " Gaius and the Grand Cameo of Paris," in *J. R. S.*, XXVI (1936), 152-160.

Bernouilli, J. J., *Römische Ikonographie*, Stuttgart, 1882-1897.

Borghesi, B., *Œuvres Complètes*, Paris, 1862.

Cary, E., *Dio's Roman History*, VII (Loeb Classical Library), London, 1924.

Charlesworth, M. P., *Trade Routes and Commerce of the Roman Empire*, second edition, revised, Cambridge, 1926.

———, *Five Men: Character Studies from the Roman Empire*, Martin Classical Lectures, VI, Cambridge, Mass., 1936.

———, " Tiberius," chapter XIX in *C. A. H.*, X, Cambridge, 1934.

———, " The Virtues of a Roman Emperor: Propaganda and the Creation of Belief," The Raleigh Lecture on History, 1937, in *Proceedings of the British Academy*, XXIII (1937), 105-133.

———, " Providentia and Aeternitas," in *Harv. Theol. Rev.* XXIX (1936), 107-132.

———, " The Banishment of the Elder Agrippina," in *C. P.*, XVII (1922), 260 f.

Ciaceri, E., *Tiberio Successore di Augusto*, Milan, 1934.

Cortellini, N., "A proposito di alcune date incerte nell' ultimo decennio del regno di Tiberio," in *Riv. Stor. Ant.*, III (1898), 15-22.

Curtius, L., " Ikonographische Beiträge zum Porträt der römischen Republik und der julisch-claudischen Familie, VI," in *Röm. Mitt.*, XLIX (1934), 119-156.

Dessau, H., *Geschichte der römischen Kaiserzeit*, II, i, Berlin, 1926.

Espérandieu, E., *Recueil Général des bas-reliefs, statues et bustes de la Gaule romaine*, III, Paris, 1910.

Frank, T., " The Financial Crisis of 33 A.D.," in *A.J.P.*, LVI (1935), 336-341.

Furneaux, H., *The Annals of Tacitus*, I, second edition, Oxford, 1896.

Gagé, J., " Un manifeste dynastique de Caligula," in *R.E.A.*, XXXVII (1935), 165-184.

———, " Divus Augustus," in *Rev. Arch.*, XXXIV (1931), 11-41.

Gardthausen, V., " Drusus Julius Caesar," in P.W., X, 431-434.

Gelzer, M., " Tiberius Julius Caesar," in P.W., X, 478 ff.

Gerber, A., and A. Greef, *Lexicon Taciteum*, Leipzig, 1903.

Hammond, M., *The Augustan Principate in Theory and Practice during the Julio-Claudian Period*, Cambridge, Mass., 1933.

Heiss, A., *Déscription Générale des Monnaies Antiques de l'Espagne*, Paris, 1870.

Hirschfeld, O., *Kleine Schriften*, Berlin, 1913.

———, " Zur annalistischen Anlage des taciteischen Geschichtswerkes," in *Hermes*, XXV (1890), 365-373.

Hohl, E., " Zu den Testamenten des Augustus," in *Klio*, XXX (1937), 323-342.

———, " Wann hat Tiberius das Prinzipat übernommen," in *Hermes*, LXVIII (1933), 106-113.

Huelsen, Chr., " Neue Inschriften von Forum Romanum," in *Klio*, II (1902), 227-283.

———, " Anagnia," in P.W., I, 2024 f.

———, " Calagna," in P.W., III, 1327.

Imhoof-Blumer, F., *Porträtköpfe auf römischen Münzen der Republik und der Kaiserzeit*, Leipzig, 1922.

Jackson, J., *Tacitus: The Annals* (Loeb Classical Library), London, 1931, 1937.

Jacoby, F., *Fragmente der griechischen Historiker*, II B, Berlin, 1929.

Kornemann, E., *Neue Dokumente zum lakonischen Kaiserkult*, Breslau, 1929.

Kroll, W., " Germanicus Julius Caesar," in P. W., X, 435 ff.

Leuze, O., " Bericht über die Literatur zur römischen Chronologie (Kalender und Jahrzählung) in den Jahren 1901-1928," in *Jahresber. Altertumswiss.*, CCXXVII (1930), 97-138.

Marsh, F. B., *The Reign of Tiberius*, Oxford, 1931.

———, " Tacitus and Aristocratic Tradition," in *C. P.*, XXI (1926), 289-310.

———, " Roman parties in the Reign of Tiberius," in *A. H. R.*, XXXI (1926), 233-250.

Marx, F. A., " Untersuchungen zur Komposition und zu den Quellen von Tacitus Annalen," in *Hermes*, LX (1925), 74-93.

Mattingly, H., " The Roman ' Virtues,' " in *Harv. Theol. Rev.*, XXX (1937), 103-117.

Mommsen, Th., *The Provinces of the Roman Empire*, translated by W. P. Dickson, London, 1909.

———, *Gesammelte Schriften*, Berlin, 1905-1913.

———, *Römisches Staatsrecht*, Leipzig, 1887-1888.

———, " Das augustische Festverzeichniss von Cumae," in *Hermes*, XVII (1882), 631-643.

Mowat, R., " Bronzes remarquables de Tibère, de son fils, de ses petit-fils et de Caligula," in *Rev. Num.*, ser. 4, XV (1911), 335-351.

Nipperdey, K., *P. Cornelius Tacitus*, I, eleventh edition, revised by G. Andresen, Berlin, 1915.

Ollendorf, L., " Livia Julia," in P. W., XIII, 924-927.

Oppolzer, Th. von, *Canon der Finsternisse*, Vienna, 1887.

Pappano, A. E., "Agrippa Postumus," in *C. P.*, XXXVI (1941), 30-45.

Parker, H. M. D., *The Roman Legions*, Oxford, 1928.

Platner, S. B., and T. Ashby, *A Topographical Dictionary of Ancient Rome*, Oxford, 1929.

Radin, M., *Marcus Brutus*, New York, 1939.

Ritterling, H., " Legio," in P. W., XII, 1211 ff.

160   STUDIES IN THE REIGN OF TIBERIUS

Rogers, R. S., *Criminal Trials and Criminal Legislation under Tiberius*, American Philological Association Monographs, VI, Middletown, 1935.

——, "Lucius Arruntius," in *C. P.*, XXVI (1931), 31-45.

——, "The Date of the Banishment of the Astrologers," in *C. P.*, XXVI (1931), 203 f.

——, "Two Criminal Cases Tried before Drusus Caesar," in *C. P.*, XXVII (1932), 75-79.

——, "The Conspiracy of Agrippina," in *T. A. P. A.*, LXII (1931), 141-168.

——, "Der Prozess des Cotta Messalinus," in *Hermes*, LXVIII (1933), 121-123.

——, "Drusus Caesar's Tribunician Power," in *A. J. P.*, LXI (1940), 457-459.

——, "Tiberius' Reversal of an Augustan Policy," in *T. A. P. A.*, LXXI (1940), 532-536.

Rolfe, J. C., *Suetonius*, I, revised (Loeb Classical Library), London, 1928.

Rostovtzeff, M., "L'Empereur Tibère et le Culte Impériale," in *Rev. Hist.*, CLXIII (1930), 1-26.

Schanz, M., *Geschichte des römischen Literatur*, 2 Teil, fourth edition, revised by C. Hosius, München, 1935.

Schmidt, L., "Das Regnum Vannianum," in *Hermes*, XLVIII (1913), 292-295.

Schulz, O. Th., *Die Rechtstitel und Regierungsprogramme auf römischen Kaisermünzen*, Paderborn, 1925.

Schwarz, E., "Ueber das Reich des Vannius," in *Sudeta*, VIII (1931), 145.

——, "Wo lag das Swebenreich des Vannius?" in *Forsch. u. Fortschr.*, IX (1933), 35.

Scott, K., "Drusus Nicknamed 'Castor,'" in *C. P.*, XXV (1930), 155-161.

——, "The *Diritas* of Tiberius," in *A. J. P.*, LIII (1932), 139-151.

——, "Tiberius' Refusal of the title 'Augustus,'" in *C. P.*, XXVII (1932), 43-50.

Scott, K., and R. S. Rogers, "The Crisis of A. D. 33," in *The Clevelander*, VI (1931/2), No. 10, pp. 7, 18.

Seyrig, H., "Inscriptions de Gythion," in *Rev. Arch.*, XXIX (1929), 84-106.

Shipley, F. W., *Velleius Paterculus* (Loeb Classical Library), London, 1924.

Spengel, A., "Zur Geschichte des Kaisers Tiberius," in *Sitzb. k. b. Akad. z. Münch.*, VI (1903), Heft 1, 3-63.

Stein, A., "Maroboduus," in P. W., XIV, 1907-1910.

Steup, J., "Eine Umstellung im zweiten Buche der Annalen des Tacitus," in *Rh. M.*, XXIV (1869), 72-80.

Stuart, M., "Tacitus and the Portraits of Germanicus and Drusus," in *C. P.*, XXXV (1940), 64-67.

Sutherland, C. H. V., "Two 'Virtues' of Tiberius: a Numismatic Contribution to the History of his Reign," in *J. R. S.*, XXVIII (1938), 129-140.

Syme, R., *The Roman Revolution*, Oxford, 1939.

———, "Lentulus and the Origin of Moesia," in *J. R. S.*, XXIV (1934), 113-137.

Syme, R., and R. G. Collingwood, "The Northern Frontiers from Tiberius to Nero," chapter XXIII in *C. A. H.*, X, Cambridge, 1934.

Taylor, L. R., "Tiberius' Refusals of Divine Honors," in *T. A. P A.*, LX (1929), 87-101.

Vulić, N., "Illyricum," in P. W., IX, 1085-1088.

Weinstock, S., "Römische Reiterparade," in *Studi e Materiali di Storia delle Religioni*, XIII (1937), 10-24.

Wissowa, G., "Personifikationen abstrakter Begriffe," chapter 54, in *Religion und Kultus der Römer*, second edition, München, 1912.

INDEX OF PASSAGES CITED

Coins

INSCRIPTIONS

AUTHORS

INDEX

171